A Field Guide

YOU AND YOUR
SEWING MACHINE

*A Sewist's Guide to Troubleshooting, Maintenance,
Tips & Techniques*

Bernie Tobisch

C&T PUBLISHING

Text and photography copyright © 2018 by Bernie Tobisch

Photography copyright © 2018 by C&T Publishing, Inc.

Publisher: Amy Marson

Creative Director: Gailen Runge

Acquisitions Editor: Roxane Cerda

Managing Editor: Liz Aneloski

Editor: Lynn Koolish

Technical Editor: Debbie Rodgers

Cover/Book Designer: April Mostek

Production Coordinator: Tim Manibusan

Production Editor: Alice Mace Nakanishi

Photo Assistant: Mai Yong Vang

Photography by Bernie Tobisch, unless otherwise noted below

Style photography by Lucy Glover and Mai Yong Vang on page 3 and
the top left of pages 9, 29, 43, 67, 79, 98, 116, 122, 128, and cover

Published by C&T Publishing, Inc., P.O. Box 1456, Lafayette, CA 94549

Library of Congress Cataloging-in-Publication Data
Names: Tobisch, Bernie, 1953- author.
Title: You and your sewing machine : a sewist's guide to troubleshooting,
maintenance, tips & techniques / Bernie Tobisch.
Description: Lafayette, CA : C&T Publishing, Inc., 2018. | Includes index.
Identifiers: LCCN 2017046833 | ISBN 9781617455810 (soft cover)
Subjects: LCSH: Machine sewing. | Sewing machines.
Classification: LCC TT713 .T62 2018 | DDC 646.2/044--dc23
LC record available at https://lccn.loc.gov/2017046833

Printed in China

10 9 8 7 6 5 4 3 2 1

Acknowledgments

I would like to thank my wife, Shelley, who has been there through thick and thin. It's not easy living and working with someone, and she has managed to stick with me. Her patience, her enthusiasm, her work ethic, and her rose-colored goggles have been an immeasurable help to me. I'm looking forward to the next twenty years of adventure!

Thank you also to our great clientele. You have become family, and I appreciate your support more than I can say!

To all the shop owners with whom it's been my pleasure to work, thank you.

Last but definitely not least, to Glen Zoerb, who hired me into this business and taught me a thing or two, my heartfelt thanks!

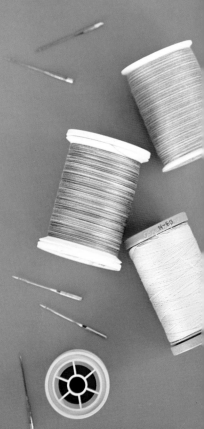

CONTENTS

PROBLEMS AND HOW TO FIX THEM   66

INTRODUCTION

I have been a sewing machine technician for 42 years and have enjoyed every minute of it. I couldn't have found a better career to match my personality and skill set. I have had the opportunity to work on every kind of sewing machine from 200-needle mattress quilters to the latest household computerized embroidery machines.

For the last 20 years, my focus has been on household machines. Along with my wife, Shelley, I have taught many hundreds of classes. She teaches the techniques, and I relate them to the sewing machine. This has worked very well and has been a lot of fun for us.

Over the years, I have come to understand and appreciate that most sewists have a very strong relationship with their sewing machine. The connection is not like one with a toaster, microwave oven, or dishwasher. This is much more personal. I've heard it said that in a fire, the sewing machine would be the first item to be saved. I have seen this relationship be the source of much joy and the cause of many tears.

In our many classes, I have started to see myself as somewhat of a relationship counselor and always do my best to reestablish trust and understanding. But at times where there were irreconcilable differences between sewist and machine, I have also had to facilitate separation and divorce.

My goal with this book is to help you gain a better understanding of your sewing machine—its needs and what it is trying to communicate to you.

I hope that this new understanding will allow you and your machine to become best friends. I have tried to include enough styles of sewing machine so you find one that is similar to yours; but as always, the manual that came with your machine should be the final authority. If you don't have a manual, many manufacturers have downloads available from their websites.

HOW TO USE THIS BOOK

This book is divided into three sections:

Getting to Know Your Sewing Machine

· Take a look at Sewing Systems and Hook Types (page 11) to identify what type of sewing system your machine has—knowing this will allow you to apply specific information and advice about your particular type of sewing machine.

· Look through the rest of this section for information about sewing machine features.

Maintaining Your Good Relationship

· Refer to this section when you have questions about the best sewing machine foot to use in specific sewing situations.

· Read through Cleaning and Lubricating (page 43) to see what maintenance you should be performing regularly on your machine.

· Take a look at Other Maintenance (page 63) to see what applies to your machine(s).

Problems and How to Fix Them

· This section will help you address problems that occur as you are using your machine.

· The Troubleshooting Guide (page 137) is a great reference and will refer you to appropriate information in the book to address specific common problems.

GETTING TO KNOW YOUR SEWING MACHINE

Knowing your machine can be the difference between a happy experience or a frustrating one. This section will help you understand how things work, and that knowledge will allow you to focus more on your project and less on problems and issues with the sewing machine.

MACHINE
FEATURES

Sewing machines range from wonderfully simple—the old Singer Featherweights, for example—to the new high-tech computerized models. Regardless of the type of machine you have, the basic sewing functionality is the same: The needle takes the top thread down below the needle plate (page 17), where the hook (next page) grabs it and takes it around the bobbin thread. That creates the stitch. The feed dogs transport and release the fabric to give an even stitch length. This chapter focuses on the mechanisms that perform these functions.

How a Stitch Is Formed

The following photos use enlarged mock-ups of the needle, thread, and fabric to clearly show how stitches are formed on a sewing machine.

When the needle pushes down through fabric, it takes with it a certain amount of thread. As the needle comes back up, the thread is pinched between the back of the needle and the fabric. This creates a loop above the eye.

When the needle comes back up 2–2.5 mm, the tip of the hook grabs this loop. As the top thread is pulled around the bobbin case, the take-up lever pulls the excess thread back up and snugly into the fabric. In the photo, my finger takes the place of the tip of the hook.

Threaded sewing machine needle

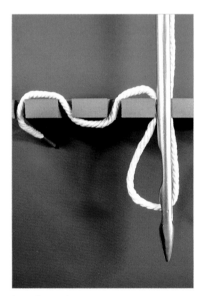

Loop formed

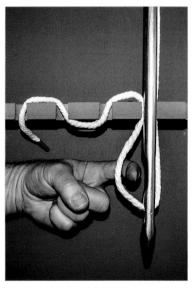

Hook grabbing top thread loop

Sewing Systems and Hook Types

The sewing system that creates the stitches is the combination of the hook and bobbin case, and there are many designs. (The hook is the metal part that revolves around the bobbin case. It is responsible for picking the thread up from the back of the needle and pulling it over the top of the bobbin to form a knot with the bobbin thread.)

Manufacturers have their signature styles. Below are the popular versions. One should look like yours. Look at the photos and make a note of which type of sewing system your machine has for future reference and troubleshooting.

For more information on bobbin cases, see Damage to the Bobbin Case (page 82).

Oscillating or CB system with hook and bobbin case

Industrial-style vertical rotary with hook and bobbin case

Drop-in bobbin horizontal rotary with hook and bobbin case

Large vertical rotary with hook and bobbin case

Floating vertical rotary with hook and bobbin case

High-speed rear-facing large vertical rotary with hook and bobbin case combined

Mechanical versus Electronic versus Computerized

I am often asked what the difference is between these types of sewing machines. The following are my definitions.

Mechanical Sewing Machine

A mechanical sewing machine has no circuitry in it. The stitch patterns are formed by cams and followers. These cams or discs may be built in, insertable, or both. They have bumps on them, and as they turn, the followers are moved by the bumps and in turn move the needle to its proper position in the stitch as you sew.

The motor is AC (alternating current; see Sewing Machine Motors, page 15). This is the same as your household current. The machine may have a rheostat or electronic foot control (see Foot Controls, page 20).

These are the vintage sewing machines or today's lower-end offerings.

Mechanical sewing machines have no automatic needle stop, and they stop randomly in their cycle when you take your foot off the controller. When you stop, be sure to turn the handwheel toward you until the needle has barely started on its downward path. This will help prevent thread nests upon starting.

Cams and followers for various stitches

Electronic Sewing Machines

This type of machine forms stitches using cams and followers, just like a mechanical version. It uses a minimal amount of circuitry to control the power to the motor and often comes with an electronic foot control (page 21). The motor may be AC or DC (direct current; see Sewing Machine Motors, page 15). There may be needle-up and -down features (page 20) and LED indicators for stitch settings.

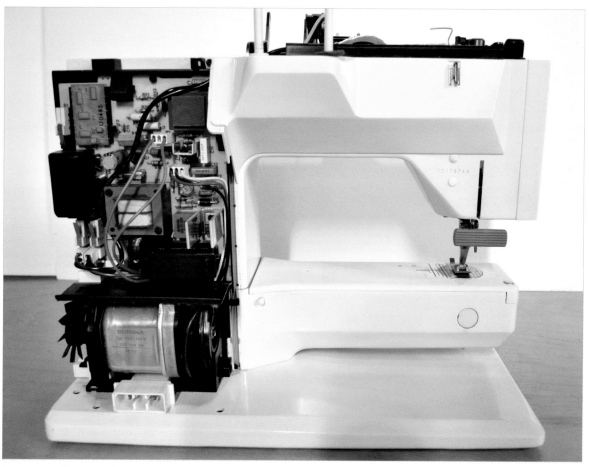

Power control board on electronic machine

Computerized Sewing Machines

A computerized sewing machine has no cams for creating stitches; instead, the needle and feed dog positions for each stitch are stored in a chip. The information for each position is sent to stepping motors that control the needle bar and the feed dogs. A stepping motor is a small motor run on magnetic impulse—there is one for stitch length and one for stitch width. As you change the length and width of your stitch, you change the voltage to the motors and the position of the needle bar or the feed dogs to their correct positions. Because each stitch is just a matter of programming, and not cramming another disc or cam into the machine, there can be a larger variety of stitches.

Computerized sewing machines can be put into a number of categories. There are push-button machines and touchscreen machines. Some are sewing machines and some are sewing and embroidery machines. There are also stand-alone embroidery machines.

One of the great features of this type of machine is that the stitches are programmed in with an optimal default stitch length and width. This can make it easier for the sewist to operate the machine.

Computerized sewing machines also have memories, where stitches that have been altered or grouped can be stored and retrieved as needed. As a rule, these machines have DC motors, which provide better control at slow speeds (see DC Motors, page 16).

Many of today's computerized sewing machines have sensors that stop the machine if the top thread breaks. This is very helpful if your machine is embroidering and the thread breaks when you are not in the room. Another great feature is the low-bobbin warning found on these machines.

Inside view of computerized machine

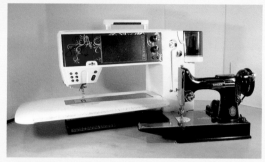
Sewing Machine Motors

Two types of motors power sewing machines. One is an AC (alternating current) motor; the other is a DC (direct current) motor.

AC Motors

The AC motor uses power as it comes from your wall outlet. The voltage will depend on the part of the world you live in.

AC motor

These motors last a very long time. When you take an older machine with this type of motor to the shop for maintenance, the sewing machine technician should check the motor brushes for wear.

Motor brushes

The downside of these motors is that they do not have very much power at low speed. That means the sewing machine can labor when you need to sew slowly. This can be a problem when sewing over dense fabric or many layers. They can be so weak that when you start to sew, you might have to help by turning the handwheel by hand. Manufacturers have overcome some of this problem with circuitry, but many lower-end sewing machines suffer from this lack of power.

DC Motors

DC (direct current) motors do not use the power as it comes from your wall outlet—it needs to be converted from AC to DC and regulated to the appropriate voltage for the motor used. This requires what is commonly referred to as a power circuit board. Most mid- to top-end sewing machines have DC motors. Their advantages can make them desirable.

DC motor

DC MOTOR ADVANTAGES

If you are the type of sewist who likes control and precision, then a machine that features a DC motor is for you.

- DC motors offer much more piercing and feeding power at slow speeds. This makes climbing over that seam in a pair of jeans much less daunting. Some brands use sensors that can detect the amount of resistance the needle is meeting and instantly provide more power to help push through.

- DC motors are easier to use at slow speeds. A light touch on the foot control, and the machine will start. No need to help the handwheel.

- Some manufacturers have devised ways to meter power to these motors that allow them to stop the instant you take your foot off the controller. This is a feature that gives you far more precision and control over your sewing. Some machines allow half-stitch by half-stitch forward and reverse movements. This puts you firmly in the driver's seat!

SAFETY

With all that available power, manufacturers needed to create fail-safes to protect the machine and motor if a needle hits something solid.

This has been accomplished in two ways. Some machines use fuses that burn out when the motor can no longer turn. This does offer the required protection, but the fuses are not easily accessible for replacement. This means a trip to the shop. A more sophisticated method uses sensors that shut down the motor when too much resistance is met. Once the cause of this resistance is removed, the machine goes about its business again.

Needle Plates

Today's sewing machines have many great features that sewists couldn't even have imagined 25 years ago. Among these is the ability to sew much wider stitches. Some brands offer stitches that are 7 mm wide; others are 9 mm wide. This feature means that manufacturers had to widen the opening in the needle plate and increase the distance between the feed dogs to accommodate these wider stitches.

As with many things, you can find pros and cons. The increased stitch width gives beautiful decorative stitches. Straight stitches can be sewn in many more needle positions, giving more options for topstitching.

On the down side, fine fabrics can be pushed down into the needle plate by the needle. Starting a seam right at the edge of a fabric can be more difficult. Stitching at the point of a triangle can cause the fabric to be eaten.

Having the feed dogs farther apart means that there will be more situations where you may not be using the total feeding capability of the machine. An example of this might be piecing with a ¼˝ seam allowance.

To ensure that you get the most out of this great feature, manufacturers have made needle plates of varying widths.

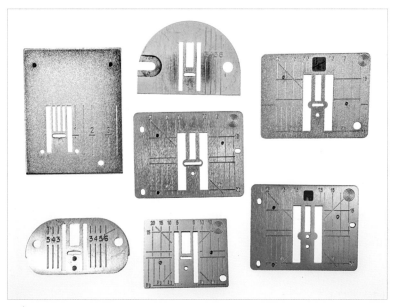

Various needle plates

For straight stitching on fine fabrics and for generally more precision, there is the straight-stitch plate. The small hole does not allow fabric to be pushed down inside. This plate is great for fine fabrics and will increase your precision. When the needle point meets the fabric, it will penetrate without moving it. The less the fabric moves, the better the stitching and the more accurate the feeding.

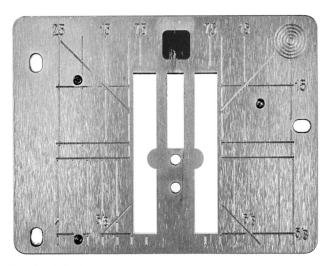

Straight-stitch plate

On a cautionary note: If you select a stitch that has any width to it or an alternate needle position, the needle can make contact with the plate. This will break the needle and possibly damage the needle plate ... not to mention, it's annoying.

To solve this problem, some machines have sensors built in to override the width settings. Some machines allow you to tell them which plate is currently being used. This is a great feature when multiple plates are available. These machines limit the stitch width and needle position to the maximum allowed by the plate.

Another idea that was invented many years ago but has recently made a comeback is a needle plate that converts from zigzag to straight stitch. This is a time-saver because you do not have to change anything.

The caution here is that if you have a needle strike on these plates, the piece that has the small opening can be easily bent. In its bent state, it won't slide out completely and snugly into place when called upon. At best, the needle will be deflected and stitches will skip. At worst, the needle will strike again and cause damage. It is a nice feature, but check it regularly, especially after you break a needle.

Damaged needle plate

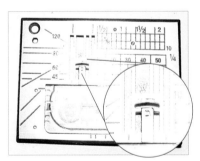

Needle plate with straight-stitch opening retracted

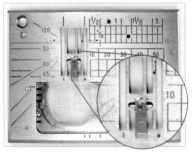

Needle plate with straight-stitch opening extended

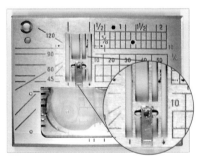

Needle plate with damaged extension

Some brands of machines with wider stitching also make a narrower-zigzag needle plate. This plate allows you to work with zigzag stitches on finer fabrics. It's a great way to overcome puckering and shifting of fabric that might normally occur when using the wider plate.

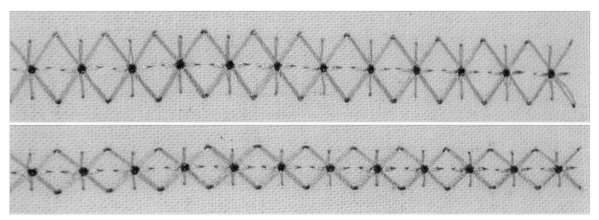

Decorative stitching with wide and narrow opening

Knee Lifters (Free-Hand Systems)

This is a great invention that has made it into the mainstream. Using your knee, you can lift the presser foot or drop it at the beginning of a seam. Combined with the needle-stop down, you can easily pivot when topstitching or appliquéing. This is a real time-saver. Some of these systems are mechanical, and some have an electronic assist. One style drops the feed dogs when you activate it. This, combined with the extra lift, makes it easy to slip bulky fabric under the foot. The feed dogs reengage on the next stitch.

If you sewed in the past with a machine that had its speed controlled with a knee lever, the lifter might take a little getting used to, but it is worth it!

One thing to remember is that when you lift the foot with the knee lift, it also separates the tension discs for you. This means that if you inadvertently rest your leg on the lever as you are sewing, you may get loops on the back of your fabric.

Knee resting on knee lifter

Foot Controls

The foot control is like the accelerator pedal of your car and controls the speed of your machine.

There are two types of foot controls on the market. One is electronic and has circuitry inside it. The other is a rheostat. It can be good to understand the difference.

Note: It is important to know that some foot controls are designed to work only with their own sewing machines. These machines may provide special features, such as raising and lowering the needle or presser foot. Some may engage the thread cutter and lift the foot. Others may be programmable and allow the sewist to choose what features they engage. These foot controls should always be replaced with the exact same one.

Foot control with needle-up/-down feature

Rheostat

This type of controller has one or two tubes with a number of small carbon wafers in them. When you step on the pedal, you introduce current to the wafers. As you push down harder, these wafers compress together and are able to conduct more electricity, thereby increasing power to the motor and increasing speed.

Inside of rheostat foot control

The main issue with this style is heat buildup at slow speed. When you use light pressure on the pedal, the carbon wafers are not compressed together tightly, leaving space in between. Electricity arcs across these spaces and creates heat. You can sometimes hear these little sparks. You will probably feel the heat. There is no danger; it's just how they are designed.

If you shake one of these controls and hear something rattling around or see a piece of a wafer falling out, I would replace it. If it gets extremely hot, I would also get rid of it. Another issue is getting only high speed as the control gets older. This can be because the metal contacts are burned or carbon wafers have disintegrated. Sometimes this condition can be fixed by a sewing machine technician. When the time comes to do this, you might consider replacement with an electronic foot control.

Electronic

In this style of control, the carbon wafers are replaced by electronic circuitry.

This is simple circuitry designed to provide smooth and even power to the motor at all speeds without arcing and heat. They are very inexpensive and make a great replacement for that old rheostat when it gives up.

Some of these circuit boards have a fine adjustment for setting slow speed.

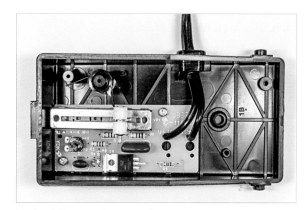

Inside of electronic foot control

ERRATIC SPEED

Occasionally the electronic foot control can give an uneven speed. This is especially true if you like to sew at a certain speed. If this happens, unplug the control and press it up and down through its entire range of motion for a minute. This removes grease and debris from the resistor and often solves the problem.

Early versions of electronic controllers, starting from the 1970s, may no longer provide control at slow speed. These have a very inexpensive capacitor that can be replaced to solve the problem. A knowledgeable sewing machine technician will be aware of this.

Bobbins

Styles of Bobbin Cases

Oscillating or CB bobbin case and adjustment screw

Industrial-style vertical rotary bobbin case and adjustment screw

Horizontal rotary drop-in bobbin case and adjustment screw

Self-winding bobbin case and adjustment screw

Newer-style self-winding bobbin case and adjustment screw

Metal drop-in bobbin case and adjustment screw

Modern, large vertical rotary bobbin case and adjustment screw

Modern, large vertical rotary bobbin case and adjustment tab

Bobbin Sensors

A wonderful feature of many sewing machines is the low-bobbin indicator. You never need to run out of thread mid-seam again! Some things can interfere with the proper operation of these sensors.

When your bobbin is full, a beam between an emitter and a receiver is interrupted. When the bobbin is nearly empty, the beam is completed and you receive a message that the bobbin is going to run out.

Some systems are sophisticated enough to give you percentages of thread left. These usually have specially marked bobbins. Some of these bobbins may have a series of small mirrors; others have specially lined-up slots.

Some drop-in bobbin systems have a mechanical device that is moved into the bobbin to detect the presence of thread.

For more information and cleaning instructions, see Bobbin Sensors (page 52).

Feed Dogs

An important part of the workings of a sewing machine are the feed dogs. They are responsible for the precise movement of the fabric: forward, reverse, and in newer machines, sideways.

As the machine turns, the feed dogs go through their cycle. While the needle is out of the fabric, they transport the fabric. As the needle enters the fabric, they drop below the needle plate and return to their starting point. When you engage reverse on the machine, they reverse their cycle and move the fabric in the opposite direction. As you select different stitch lengths, you change the distance that the feed dogs travel above the plate, thus altering the size of the stitch.

Types of Feed Dogs

Most feed dogs are made of metal and have sharp teeth to give good gripping power.

Metal feed dogs

Some machines have rubberized feed dogs without any teeth. These are susceptible to damage and do not hold up very well. The good news is that they can be replaced with aftermarket metal versions. If your machine is not feeding well and has rubberized feed dogs, inspect them for missing chunks. A sewing machine technician should replace these, as precise alignment is required.

Rubber feed dogs

BOX FEED VERSUS ELLIPTICAL FEED

Manufacturers have designed the type of movement of feed dogs in basically two ways: box feed and elliptical feed. To find out what type of feed dogs your machine has, ask your sewing machine technician or take a look at how the feed dogs operate without any fabric so you can see them (it may help to take the presser foot off as well for a better view). This information is especially helpful if you are not happy with your stitch quality.

In the **box feed** system, the feed dogs rise the full distance above the needle plate before moving the fabric. They stay at that height for the full distance of transport before dropping below the needle plate as the needle enters the fabric. This ensures very even feeding of the fabric.

In the **elliptical feed** system, the feed dogs are already trying to move the fabric before they are all the way up. They are also already dropping before the needle enters the fabric. This makes it more likely to get uneven stitch length and may give more difficulty climbing seams.

Dropping the Feed Dogs

Many sewing machines give you the option of dropping the feed dogs. Some of the vintage machines have different height settings for them. This ability to lower the feed dogs out of the way is very useful to free-motion quilters and thread painters. With the feed dogs out of the way, they will no longer try to move the fabric. This also gives a smoother surface at the needle plate and allows the fabric a more unimpeded flow.

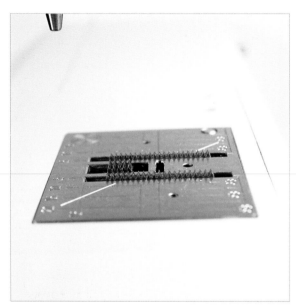

Feed dogs up

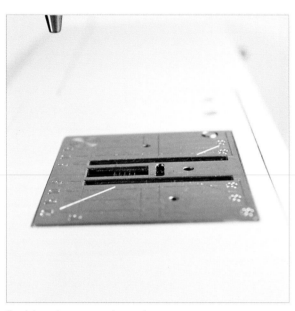

Feed dogs down, smoother surface

Be aware that when you reengage the feed dogs, you may not see them immediately pop up above the surface of the needle plate. On most modern machines, they will spring into action as you take the first stitch.

Check your user manual to see where to raise and lower your machine's feed dogs.

QUESTIONS TO ASK WHEN BUYING A NEW SEWING MACHINE

I am including this chapter because I have seen many broken relationships between sewists and their sewing machines—such as machines that were bought to sew heavy-duty fabrics but did not have enough power, machines that won't easily do free-motion work for quilters, and so on. The list is long. These relationships could have been fulfilling and lasting just by asking a few questions and, importantly, by doing some simple testing.

My list of questions and reasons, in no particular order …

Does the machine have a DC motor?

If you are looking to have precise control at slow speed and want powerful needle penetration of dense fabrics, this is a must (see Sewing Machine Motors, page 15). Most new machines, especially computerized and electronic ones, have DC motors. *Bottom line:* Try out the machine and make sure you can start and sew slowly without using the handwheel to get started.

Are the feed dogs box or elliptical?

The box feed will give you a more consistent stitch length over a wide range of fabrics and better feeding of fabric, especially over seams (see Feed Dogs, page 22).

What are the increments of adjustments for length and width?

More increments give you more precise control over stitches.

What is the maximum width of stitches?

This tells you how big the opening in the needle plate is, which is important if you plan to use decorative stitching. This opening can also be a factor for precision, and you may want or need to purchase a straight-stitch plate (see Needle Plates, page 17).

What type of sewing system does the machine have? Rotary or oscillating? Drop-in or vertical bobbin? Large or small bobbin?

This may have an impact on the type of sewing you want to do. For example, oscillating is the most forgiving for free-motion. (See Sewing Systems and Hook Types, page 11.)

How fast can it sew?

If you do a lot of long seams or free-motion stitching, look for a faster machine. Most machines will sew somewhere between 750 to 1,100 stitches per minute. It's good to test-sew to see if the speed of the machine suits your sewing and goes fast enough for the work you want to do on it.

How slowly can it sew?

Many tasks require precise control at very slow speeds. This is another thing you will want to test. Make sure you can sew slowly enough to achieve the result you want. (See Sewing Machine Motors, page 15.)

Does it have mirror imaging of stitches?

I've seen quilters find out that the blanket stitch went the wrong direction on their new machine.

How well does it do free-motion?

An important consideration for quilters and thread painters. Test this out when machine shopping (see Testing the Machine, next page).

How is the motor protected from overload?

Fuse or sensor? Trip to the shop or fix at home? A sensor will reset after a needle crash; a fuse will have to be replaced in the shop. (See Sewing Machine Motors, page 15.)

Does the machine have a presser foot pressure adjustment?

This allows you to sew a wider range of fabrics without shifting. It is also necessary for ease of climbing seams. See Presser-Foot Pressure Adjustment (page 116).

Can I change the default settings of stitch length and width, needle position, and so on and save them?

This feature is a great time-saver and a way to personalize your machine.

Does it have a knee lift to raise the presser foot?

This feature is a great time-saver; no need to reach behind to lift the lever by hand (see Knee Lifters [Free-Hand Systems], page 19).

Does it have LED lighting?

A nice white light is best to illuminate the sewing area.

Can I remove the needle plate without using a screwdriver?

It is much easier and less frustrating to remove a needle plate that does not require a screwdriver (see Removing the Needle Plate, page 44).

How are the feet changed?

Find the foot attachment system that is easiest for you to use (see Using the Right Foot, page 29).

How much do the feet wobble from side to side?

This impacts directly on accuracy and is often overlooked.

Can I lower the feed dogs?

This is very important if you are planning on doing any free-motion work, such as quilting or thread painting (see Feed Dogs, page 22).

How long is the warranty? On circuit boards? Mechanical? Labor?

Not all manufacturers offer the same length of warranty on their machines. Check whether the dealer offers an extra warranty.

Is the servicing and repair work done in house?

This is a more important question than you might think. If you have a problem and it can't be fixed where you bought it, it may mean long periods without your machine. Many shops contract out service. Is the sewing machine technician trained in that brand?

Do I get lessons?

Get the most out of your sewing machine.

Are accessories for my type of sewing available for this machine?

Make sure the available accessories meet your sewing needs.

Testing the Machine

It surprises me how often someone will buy a sewing machine without testing it to see if it meets their requirements. I had a shop for many years, and very few people ever brought in the fabrics and threads they sewed with. I always appreciated when a sewist actually tried out the exact tasks they expected the machine to accomplish. It allowed me and my staff to find the best machine for the customer. We never saw it as a bother.

It is very important if you are going to be hemming jeans to bring in a hem that has been cut off and try sewing over the side seam. If you are a quilter and you want to do free-motion, satisfy yourself that the sewing machine does what you expect by trying it yourself. As a garment sewer, buttonholes will be very important. Try them in various places on an old garment. If you sew specialty fabrics, bring them with you when you test drive a machine. The same goes for specialty threads.

It is much easier to walk away before you buy the machine than it will be to keep bringing it back to the shop. It's okay if the people in the shop think you are picky. That's better than seeing you frustrated when the machine doesn't do what you want it to.

Buying Online versus from a Dealer

This question comes up often. Online purchases can sometimes save a few dollars, and that can make them attractive. However, buying a sewing machine is not like buying a toaster. Most people will require help to familiarize themselves with their new machine. That's hard to do by phone. Many computerized machines get firmware updates. Dealers are usually happy to do these for you. What if you need mechanical updates? If you experience a problem with your new online purchase, you will need to send it back to have it rectified—either that or take it to the dealer you bypassed.

Where I can see buying online is when the product you want is not available locally or the dealer is someone that you prefer not to do business with.

I would give a dealer an opportunity to meet the online price. Most will probably come close. If they won't, then weigh the options. Keep in mind that it costs money to have a location, provide teaching staff, and have a sewing machine technician. All these things can be a great benefit to you, even if it costs a little bit more.

MAINTAINING YOUR GOOD RELATIONSHIP

Any relationship I've been in always required a bit of work to keep things running smoothly. Oiling a squeaky wheel and smoothing out the rough spots went a long way toward harmony. It's the same with your sewing machine. A little bit here and there will keep both of you happy! I can't go into detail about each procedure a sewing machine technician goes through to service your machine, but I can offer some tips to keep things going between trips to the shop for regular maintenance.

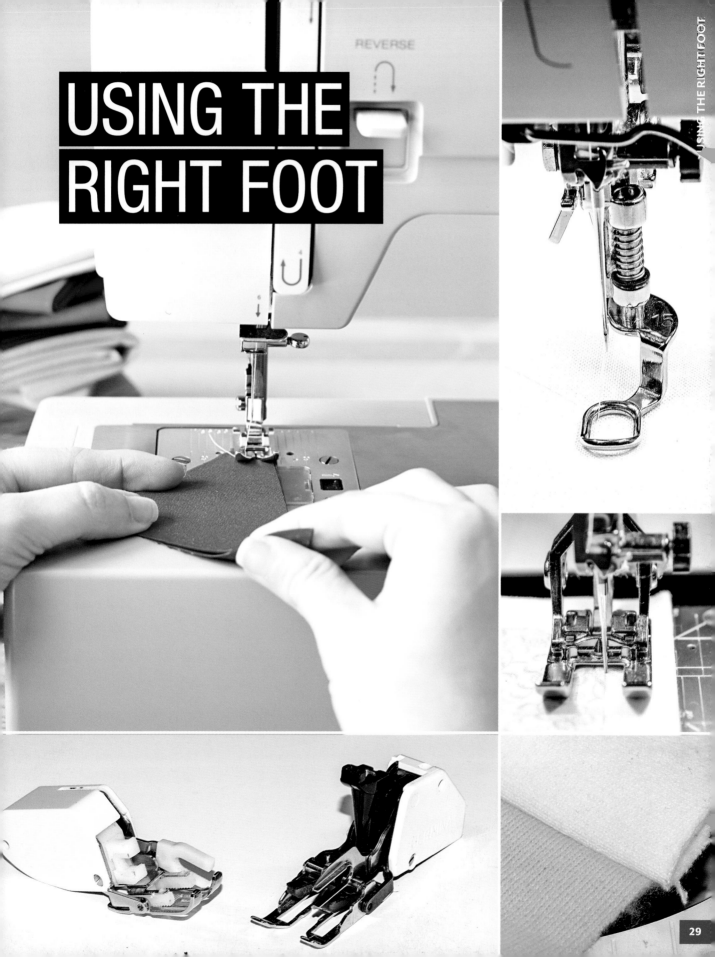

USING THE RIGHT FOOT

In this chapter, my goal is not to describe every foot and its uses, but to touch on some situations in which the right foot makes a big difference.

Embroidery or Appliqué Foot

When to Use It

The same characteristic that will cause problems for normal sewing will help give great results when this foot is used for its intended purpose. The hollow on the underside will allow a bead of satin stitching to flow through unimpeded. This gives a more consistent looking stitch without pileups or gaps. Another area where this foot does a good job is with decorative stitches or lettering. As long as the fabric is properly stabilized, it will allow good flow with heavier decorative threads and closer together stitching.

Using the open-toe version of this foot gives great visibility when appliquéing.

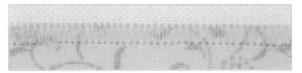

Nice satin stitch

Appliqué with open toe

When Not to Use It

Every week as I am doing repairs, I see machines on which sewists are using an embroidery foot for their normal sewing. Often the complaint is inconsistent tension or puckering fabric. This happens because the foot is designed with a hollowed-out underside.

This hollow allows the fabric to move up and down when sewing normal tasks, leading to uneven tension or skipping stitches. When doing a zigzag, it will be more likely to pucker the fabric.

Fabric lifting when sewing

Hollowed-out underside

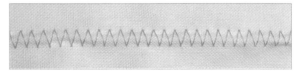

Puckered fabric from using the wrong foot

The correct foot for normal sewing is either the zigzag foot or straight stitch foot. These do not have the hollow underneath and keep downward support on the fabric. This gives better tension and helps to prevent skipped stitches.

Correct zigzag feet

Walking Foot

A walking foot is a real necessity when sewing multiple layers of fabric. It is also a great help when working with polar fleece and when there is batting involved.

The walking foot has a set of feed dogs that help to transport the top fabric at the same rate as the bottom. This eliminates the top layer from being pushed ahead and ending up much longer than the one on the bottom. When sewing a grid, it also helps get rid of puckering between rows.

A lever with a fork is placed on the needle clamp, and as the needle moves up and down, the mechanism is activated.

Walking foot installed with fork over needle clamp

Top layer growing

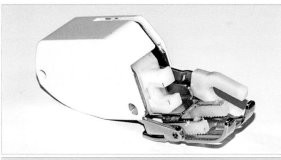

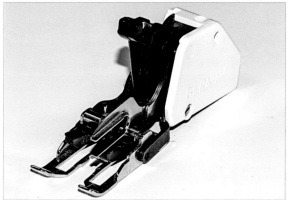

Walking feet

Puckering between rows of grid

It is helpful when buying a walking foot to make sure the feed dogs line up in position with the feed dogs of the sewing machine. This aids in feeding.

Some higher-end walking feet have exchangeable soles. This makes it possible to do a better job on a wider range of tasks.

Top layer same length when sewn with walking foot

No puckering in grid

Closed Sole

This sole provides good downward pressure on puffy fleeces and stops them from tunneling up into the opening of the foot.

Open Sole

The bar in front of the needle is cut away on this sole. This gives great visibility for appliquéing or stitching-in-the-ditch.

Walking foot with closed sole

Open sole showing visibility

Stitch-in-the-Ditch or Edge-Stitching Sole

A guide is built into this sole. It is used to run along the high side of a seam when the needle is in the center position. It makes a great stitch-in-the-ditch guide. Moving the needle position makes it into an edge-stitch foot.

Used as stitch-in-the ditch guide

Used as edge-stitch guide

Many levels of quality of walking feet are available. Do not scrimp on this important tool. The low-quality ones do not work well and fall apart in no time. Go to a knowledgeable dealer to get good advice on the best walking foot for your machine.

WALKING FOOT VERSUS BUILT-IN DUAL-FEED SYSTEM

This has been a long-running debate. The side you are on may depend on what machine you have. In my experience, the walking foot and built-in dual feed are two different tools that do different jobs very well. For many years the built-in dual feed was sold as a built-in walking foot. I believe this did a disservice to customer and dealer alike. A walking foot reaches in front of the needle and helps move fabric toward it. This eliminates the top-layer shifting that occurs when sewing with batting, for example. A dual feed moves fabric from behind the needle after it has already been sewn. It cannot transport fabric to the needle. This is a very important distinction.

I have done a great deal of testing, and my results are nearly always the same. I make a quilt sandwich about 12˝ long and 8˝ wide. (A *quilt sandwich* is two pieces of cotton fabric with a layer of batting in between.) I sew across the bottom about an inch away from the edge. I then start at the top of the piece and sew toward the line I have already sewn. I use a dual feed for the first seam and the walking foot for the second.

Dual feed

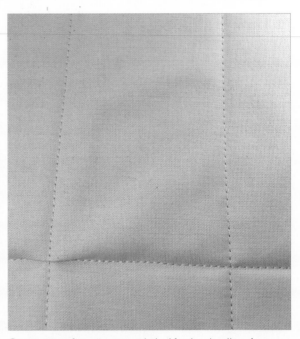
Comparison of seams sewn with dual feed and walking foot

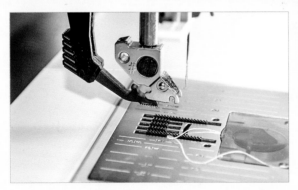
Another style of dual feed

Using the dual feed, I get a fold across the horizontal seam. With the walking foot, there is no fold. I have no stake in this, and I am certainly not being critical of the dual feed. It is a wonderful tool for great feeding of many fabrics. This has been my experience, and I have seen many people in classes with unreachable expectations for this feature.

SERVICING A WALKING FOOT

Most walking feet on the market are disposable. When they stop working, you just buy a new one. One has been made to last a long time—as far as I know, the BERNINA walking foot is the only one that can be serviced in a few easy steps to keep it running smoothly and last even longer. A sign that service is needed is that stitch length is uneven or the fabric has puckers.

1. Lift the white plastic cover over the silver screw and slide it off completely.

Lift the plastic cover.

2. Remove the two screws as indicated by the pointers.

Remove screws.

3. Put a drop of sewing machine oil at the pivot as shown by the pointer. Check to see that the springs are hooked up as they are in the photo.

Oil at the pivot.

4. Gently pull out the forked lever and oil where indicated by pointers.

Pull out lever.

5. Check that the silver bearings are turning freely; if they are not, the arm they are on may be slightly bent. Make sure they are perfectly horizontal to the walking foot body. Bend them back gently if needed. If you are worried about doing this, take the walking foot in to the dealer and have them service it.

Put a small amount of oil on the shaft of the bearings and on top of the feed dogs they rest on. Wipe off any excess—you don't want it on your fabric.

Check bearings.

6. Turn the walking foot upside down and inspect the rubber feed dogs. If there are chunks missing or grooves worn into them, they can be replaced by your dealer.

Inspect rubber feed dogs.

7. Reassemble in reverse order.

Edge-Stitch Foot

This is another foot that can make a big difference in your results. The edge-stitch foot has a guide in the center. By moving the needle position and running the layer of fabric to be edgestitched or topstitched along the guide, you can achieve perfect results. Changing needle positions will move the row of stitching to the desired distance from the edge.

A blind-hem foot can be used as an edge-stitch foot in some situations.

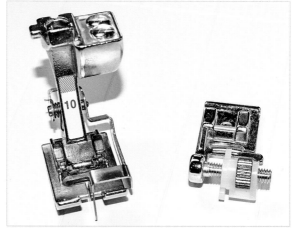

Edge-stitch foot showing guide (*left*) and adjustable blind-hem foot (*right*)

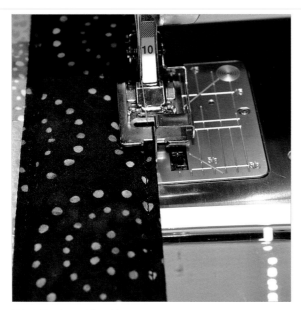

Fabric lined up with guide

Perfect result!

Patchwork or ¼˝ Foot

This foot is a must for quilters. It is designed to give the ¼˝ seam allowance that is so important for piecing the quilt top. Many styles are available for this type of foot. The one that works best for you depends on the type of machine you sew with.

Patchwork feet with and without guide

These feet come with or without a guide. A guide may help you or, as we have seen in numerous classes, it might be a hindrance. If you choose to use a guide, you might find that your seam allowance is a bit wide. This depends on the rigidity of the guide and, in part, your placement of the fabric.

You can test your seam allowance very easily.

1. Carefully cut 3 strips of fabric 1½˝ wide.

2. Line the first 2 pieces up right sides together and sew them together using a patchwork foot.

3. Press the seam to one side and sew the third piece of fabric to the other two. Press the seam to the side.

4. Now measure the middle piece of fabric. It should be exactly 1˝ wide. If it isn't precisely 1˝ wide, then you might want to change the fabric placement under the foot. If the fabric ends up too narrow and you use a guide, you might be better off without it.

This test is done with the assumption that the needle position is properly set on your sewing machine.

Markings on the Patchwork Foot

Most patchwork feet have markings on the side.

Markings on side of patchwork foot

Front mark   It's exactly ¼˝ in front of the needle. This might be helpful when you want to stop ¼˝ from the end of your fabric, such as when you're mitering binding corners.

Middle mark   It's right where the needle will enter the fabric.

Last mark   It's exactly ¼˝ behind the needle. This can be helpful if you want to start stitching ¼˝ from the beginning of the fabric.

Lining Up with the Feed Dogs

It is important when you are buying a patchwork foot that it covers the sewing machine's feed dogs as much as possible. This is particularly true of the machines that have the wider stitching capabilities and therefore the wider-apart feed dogs. If the foot does not cover at least the left feed dog, you might experience feeding difficulties.

Foot not covering feed dogs well—fabric may veer at beginning and end of seam. There may also be an issue with even stitch length, and the machine won't climb seams very well.

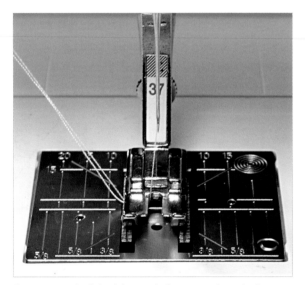

Foot covering both feed dogs—ideal scenario where the foot covers both feed dogs and gives the best feeding.

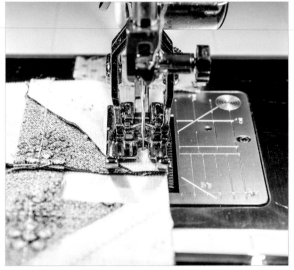

Foot covering left-side feed dog—the best compromise if you have a machine where the feed dogs are wide apart. The foot gives complete coverage over the left feed dog.

CHAIN PIECING WITH THE PATCHWORK FOOT

If you like to chain piece, it is a very good idea to lift the foot and place the fabric to the needle before you start to sew. Stop right at the end of the seam with the needle down, lift the foot slightly, and put the next piece of fabric up to the needle. Then continue sewing. This way you never sew on air or subject the underside of the foot to the scraping of the feed dogs. Your accuracy will improve, and there will be no damage to the presser foot. When the foot is scored by the feed dogs, it will stop feeding properly. The stitch length may start to vary, and the seam allowance may be inconsistent. This is easily avoided by using the chain piecing method as described.

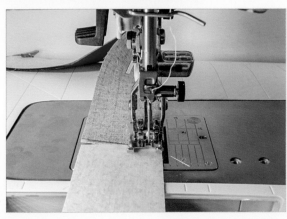

Stop with needle down and insert next piece of fabric to needle.

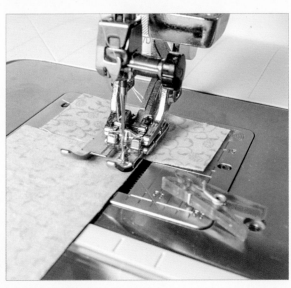

Insert fabric all the way to needle.

Damage to underside of foot

> **NOTE** *A great resource for further information is Shelley Scott-Tobisch's book* Easy Precision Piecing *(from C&T Publishing).*

Free-Motion or Darning Foot

Many types of free-motion feet are on the market. In our machine quilting classes, we have had good success with the spring type.

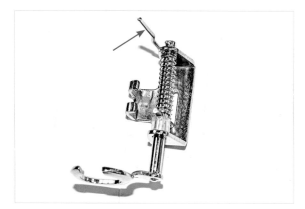

Spring-type free-motion foot

This type of foot has a bar that is lifted by the needle clamp as it moves upward.

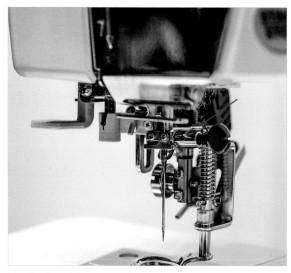

Needle clamp lifting bar on foot

When the bar is lifted, the foot lifts off the fabric to allow for ease of movement. It is important to know that the height of lift can change from machine to machine. The bar can be bent up or down carefully to give just the right amount of lift for your machine.

Some machines have clip-on feet. The free-motion foot for these machines works very well also. There is no bar to lift these feet. Instead the presser bar is lifted internally by what is called a *hopper mechanism*.

Clip-on free-motion foot

These feet do a great job and are easy to install.

Overcast Foot

I mention this foot because overcasting is something often done. The defining characteristic of this foot is the finger in the opening where the stitching takes place.

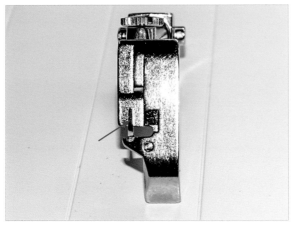

Underside of overcast foot with finger

This finger works like the stitch fingers on your serger. It holds on to a stitch or two before letting go of the thread. This has the effect of stopping the puckering on the edge of the fabric from being overcast.

Puckered fabric edge without overcast foot

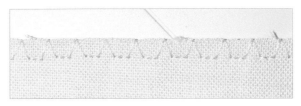

Not puckered using overcast foot

It's easy to see the value in this foot!

Stitch Regulator for Free-Motion Stitching

A few years ago, one manufacturer of household sewing machines invented a free-motion foot with a sensor that tells the machine how fast the fabric is moving underneath it. The machine's motor then changes speed to keep pace with the fabric. The benefit is a much more even stitch length when doing free-motion work.

Stitch regulator

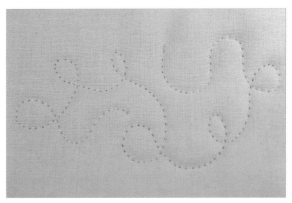

Stitches using stitch regulator

The foot will not compensate for sudden directional changes or very quick changes in speed. It does help train you to become better at any type of free-motion work. I think it is a great tool if used properly.

USING A STITCH REGULATOR

1. Plug it in.

Make sure the foot is securely plugged in. Do not hold the foot by the cable and do not unplug the foot by pulling on the cable.

Stitch regulator plugged in

Or depending on your machine:

Stitch regulator plugged in

2. Select stitch length.

Because the stitch is regulated, you can select a length that you want to work with. The default setting when plugging in the foot is 2 mm. This is a very short stitch and may not be appropriate for what you are sewing.

Also, it takes more stitches to get from point A to point B with a 2 mm stitch length.

When you first practice with this foot, it might appear to be racing. Increase the stitch length to 2.5 or 2.6 mm. This will slow things down as the machine does fewer stitches to cover the same distance, and you will feel more in control.

3. Decide to use foot control or start/stop button.

This foot works with either the foot control or the start/stop button on the front of the machine. The foot control becomes just an on/off switch when using it with the regulator. We are programmed to the idea that the foot control regulates speed, and you might try to do just that if you use it when you are first learning. Push the control down and leave it down for as long as you want the machine to run. Lift the foot when you want to

stop. If you find yourself trying to control speed with your foot, you might want to unplug it and try using the start/stop button on the front of the machine. Hold it in until the foot is activated, and then release it and start moving the fabric. When you want to stop, push the same button and the machine will stop.

4. Set the speed alarm.

It is a good idea to set the speed alarm when first learning to use this foot. Your machine sews at 900–1,100 stitches, depending on the model. As you move the fabric, the stitch length can be regulated as long as the machine is at or below its maximum speed. If you move the fabric at a speed that the machine cannot keep up with, the stitches will get longer. When you set the alarm, the machine will beep when you reach the limit at which it can regulate the stitch length. The alarm will help train you to move the fabric at the right pace.

Summary

The stitch regulator can be a great tool for some people wanting to learn free-motion. It can build your skills faster than the normal, nonregulated feet.

The tips provided here come from questions frequently asked in our classes. You should refer to your manual for in-depth instructions on the use of the stitch regulator.

CLEANING AND LUBRICATING

The Lower Part of the Machine

Keeping the hook area clean is more important than you may realize. A lot of things can happen there. The needle takes the top thread down below the needle plate, where the hook grabs it and takes it around the bobbin thread. That creates the stitch. The feed dogs transport and release the fabric to give an even stitch length. If lint is allowed to build up, these functions can be adversely affected.

Removing the Needle Plate

The first thing is to remove the needle plate. Refer to the following examples and your machine manual as needed.

Depending on your machine, do one of the following to access the bobbin case, hook, and other sewing system components.

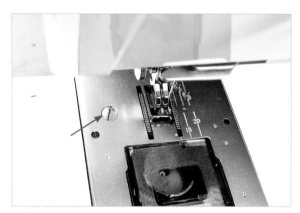

Undo screws to remove plate.

Push on marked spot and lift.

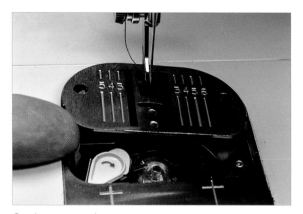

Gently pry up to release.

Lift front of plate and slide back. *Important: Drop feed dogs first.* This will prevent damage to leaf springs under plate.

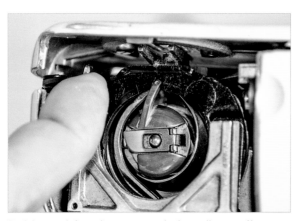

Push lever to left, and arm cover with plate will come off.

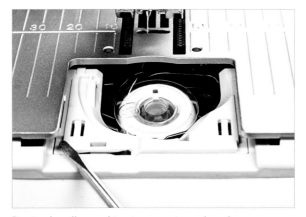

Put tip of small screwdriver into opening and gently pry up.

Slide plate forward to remove.

As you can see, there are many machine designs used by the different manufacturers. I hope you see one that resembles yours.

Taking Out the Bobbin Case and Hook

If you aren't sure what type of sewing system your machine has, refer to Sewing Systems and Hook Types (page 11).

DROP-IN BOBBIN

If you have a drop-in bobbin machine, take out the bobbin case.

Lift out bobbin case.

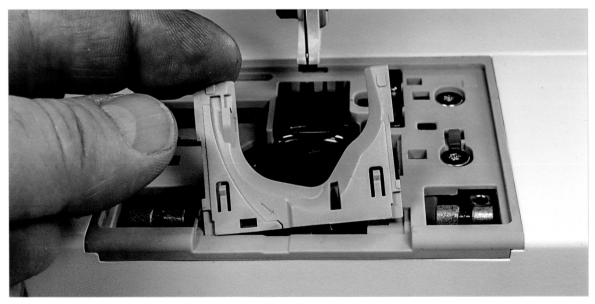

On some machines, you will need to remove retainer first.

OSCILLATING BOBBIN

For oscillating-hook machines, remove the race cover and extract the hook.

Push levers to side.

Remove race cover.

Remove hook.

or

Push silver latch to left.

Pull down race cover.

Remove hook.

LARGE VERTICAL ROTARY HOOK

To remove this hook, grab the center post and lift out and up.

Push silver latch to left.

Lower race cover.

Remove hook.

VERTICAL FLOATING HOOK

On some machines, you may need to remove some screws to access the hook.

Remove four screws.

Lift off race cover.

Remove hook.

NONREMOVABLE HOOK

On some machines, you will not be able to remove the hook.

Not removable by user

VACUUM VERSUS CANNED AIR

One of the frequently asked questions is, "Can I use canned compressed air to clean the bobbin area?" Canned air is a good product, but not the best idea for your sewing machine. When you blow lint around that area, you are sending some of it deeper into the machine. I have had to do expensive repairs for customers as a result. The lint can lodge into gears and other areas that affect feed.

Depending on the machine, the repair can cost up to the price of approximately four standard services. There is certainly no money saved by not having the sewing machine regularly serviced.

Lint and pins in feed mechanism

Gear damaged by lint

I strongly suggest that you do not use canned air or a compressor when you are cleaning the hook area. When your sewing machine technician has all the covers off, it is safe for them to use a compressor to remove lint as they will have access to all areas of the machine.

The Right Way to Clean

The best way for you to clean the hook and bobbin area is to use a soft brush and your vacuum cleaner. I sometimes buy small paintbrushes with about a 1˝-long bristle. These can get into the harder-to-get-to spots and dislodge the lint.

Most vacuums have a crevice tool and that can be helpful. You can also find very small vacuum attachments on the market that allow you to better get the nozzle into the area you are cleaning.

Clean gently and don't push the brush too far into areas you can't see into. Some machines have springs that can

Small vacuum attachments

be dislodged. These springs may be there for the thread cutter or the feed mechanisms.

If you are using a vacuum, be very sure that you have removed any loose parts. It's not fun looking through a cleaner bag or canister for missing parts.

Don't Forget the Feed Dogs

The area between the feed dogs can build up lint very quickly. When this happens, your sewing machine may not feed the fabric properly. This will show up as uneven stitch length or the inability to climb seams.

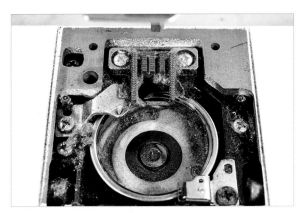

Lint buildup between feed dogs

As the feed dogs come up above the needle plate to grab the fabric, the lint starts to limit how high they can go. That lint gets compressed into felt and starts to make contact with the underside of the plate. The more that builds up, the harder it hits the plate. I have serviced many machines when even after I cleaned this felt out, the feed dogs did not come up high enough to feed the

fabric properly. This was because the mechanism was actually bent by all the contact with the needle plate, and it had to be adjusted.

You can pick out the felt by using a fine screwdriver, tweezers, or any other object that will fit.

Pick out felt.

After you have cleaned out the hook area, you can check for damage to the tip of the hook. Polish if necessary (see Smoothing Burrs on the Hook, page 80). Do the same for any damage to the bobbin case and needle plate. Now is a good time to lubricate (see Lubrication, page 57).

Bobbin Sensors

The presence of lint in the path of the beam can fool a sensor into thinking that there is thread in the bobbin. It is important to keep the area free of loose thread, debris, and lint to get optimal results.

Sensor in bobbin door

These sensors and the general area must be kept clean for the low-bobbin system to work.

Sensor under and to back of feed dogs

Special markings on bobbin

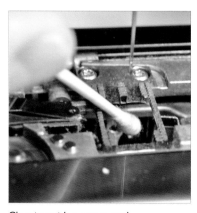

Cleaning with a cotton swab

This sensor is accessed under the needle plate. It is advisable to use a small light for visibility. I use a cotton swab to gently clean lint off the sensor. The bobbins also need to be checked once in a while to make sure the shiny rectangles are intact. If they show damage, the sensor may not work properly. If you have cleaned everything properly and the low-bobbin indicator does not function, try it with a new bobbin to see if that solves the problem.

If your machine uses this type of bobbin and the low-bobbin indicator does not work even after cleaning, it is possible that the slots do not line up properly. There is an aftermarket version of this bobbin in circulation, and many of them are not lined up.

Slotted rotary bobbin

MECHANICAL ARM LOW-BOBBIN SENSOR

The mechanical lever that detects bobbin fill is quite reliable and doesn't require much attention. Make sure it moves freely to the left and does not have threads tangled in it.

Note: Oscillating-bobbin sewing machines (see Sewing Systems and Hook Types, page 11) do not have low-bobbin indicators.

Mechanical arm

Did You Miss Anything?

Now you have a nice clean bobbin area. This does not mean that the sewing machine does not need to be serviced regularly. There is much of the machine that you do not have access to, and lint builds up in those areas as well.

Just cleaned area

Area surrounding just cleaned area

This is what lurks below! You can see pretty clearly in these photos what was left behind that you can't get at. All that lint wicks up lubricant, which then can't do its job of keeping the sewing machine running smoothly and without wear. I have had to replace parts in this area that didn't have any oil and just wore out. This is why it's important to take the machine in for service regularly.

The Upper Part of the Machine

Sewing machines vary in how much access you have to places that you can clean and oil. With some of the older machines, you can get at everything; with some of the newer ones, you can't access much of anything. This is because of the electronics involved in many of today's machines. The manufacturers don't want people to be able to damage any circuitry when maintaining their machines. That is very understandable. Having said that, there are also purely mechanical machines that don't allow access. Every brand is different. Let's look at some of the ways we can get at areas you need to keep cleaned and oiled.

Left Side Door

Some are easy—just swing the door open. Some have a screw in the side. For others, you need to loosen a screw through the top or pull down a lever at the bottom. All are easy and give you access to the head end of the sewing machine.

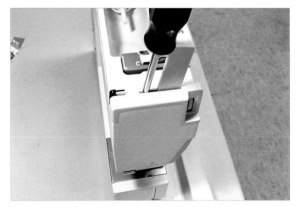

Swing open.

Screw in side

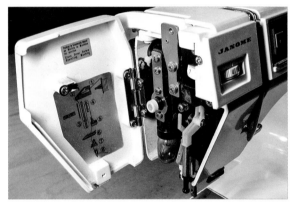

Screw through top

Pull down lever.

Top Cover

Top cover removal can be just as varied. Some machines have hinged lids that just tilt up from the front. Some have screws that need to be removed. Others just lift straight up and off.

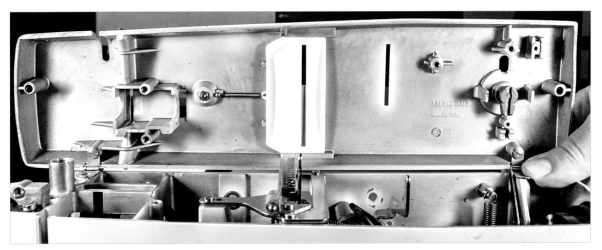

Hinged cover

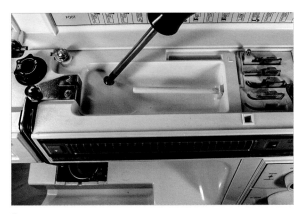

Remove screws.

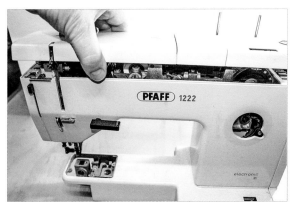

Lift straight up.

If you feel uncomfortable about removing screws, then don't worry about any of this and let your sewing machine technician take care of it for you. Don't remove anything if you are not sure about it.

After you have gained access to the area, you can use your vacuum cleaner and brush to clean up any accumulated lint and dirt. If you turn the handwheel, you might be able to reach better into some spots. You may also see stray threads stuck in some of the take-up mechanism. Try to remove these with tweezers. If you can't remove these with gentle force, then you might want to let your sewing machine technician do this at the next service.

Thread in take-up mechanism

At this stage of disassembly, it is often possible to clean the tension discs. Lift the presser foot first to separate the discs. You can "floss" between them to remove any lint, thread, or residue buildup. Do it gently, putting a piece of fabric between the discs and sliding it through, back and forth. Notice that you might have a metal separator in between. This means you have two sets of discs. Make sure to clean between both sets. If a stubborn wad of thread is stuck in there, you can use a long fine pin to help dig it out.

Flossing

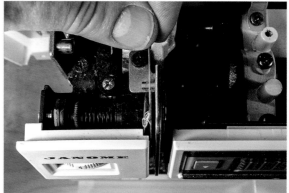

Using fine pin

After the whole area is cleaned, you can lubricate (next page) the machine. After lubrication, carefully put back all the covers.

Lubrication

Simply put, oil extends the life of your sewing machine! It makes things run smoothly and quietly by reducing friction. I have clients whose machines have many millions of stitches on them. Some of these run better than machines with far fewer stitches. Cleaning, lubrication, and regular service make all the difference.

Some sewing machines on the market have manuals in which the manufacturer states not to use oil. These machines use oil impregnated bushings and usually don't give you access. The sewing machine technician will look after any required lubrication on these products.

Check your manual for the specifics on your machine.

Using the Right Oil

Over the years I have seen sewing machines lubricated with many things. Included on the list are vegetable oil, household oils, various penetrating sprays, and moisture displacers, as well as, believe it or not, fabric fray stoppers.

Sewing machine oils are designed for their purpose. They are lightweight and don't leave a heavy residue. They are not expensive and give a great return on investment. If you are out of oil and want to lubricate your machine, it is worth a trip to the store to get a bottle of the right stuff.

Different oils for different machines

Great products, but not for machine lubrication

All these products have their place in your household—just not in your sewing machine. The easiest of them to remove was the fray stopper. I could pick it out. The vegetable oil and some of the sprays turned to glue as they evaporated and the job was not as easy.

For some sewing machines, the manufacturer specifies a particular oil. It is important to follow this recommendation. If you use regular sewing machine oil for oiling the hook in these machines, it will actually affect the stitch quality.

Stitching with right oil on hook

Stitching with wrong oil on hook

Oiling the Hook Area

If you aren't sure what type of hook your machine has, refer to Sewing Systems and Hook Types (page 11).

The number one place for the user to oil the machine is at the hook. If you have a plastic drop-in bobbin case, see Plastic Drop-In Bobbin (page 60).

In general, oiling frequency is approximately every 8–12 hours of actual sewing time, although there are exceptions. As always, refer to the manual for your machine.

VERTICAL ROTARY HOOK

These types of machines have an inner stationary basket with a post that the bobbin case fits onto. The outer moving portion revolves around this basket. It is at the place where the two interface that the oil belongs. One drop is all that is necessary.

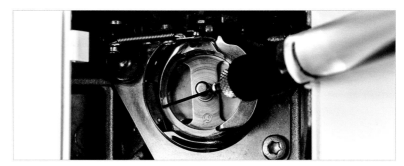

Oiling vertical rotary hook

The rattle from the hook area is the indicator that oil is required. If the machine has a stitch counter that prompts you to oil, remember to reset it, as per the manual.

OSCILLATING OR CB HOOK

These machines have a removable hook. This makes it easy to place the drop of oil in the right spot. It can be put on the race or on the edge of the hook. This edge can be accessed by opening the race gate or from under the needle plate. The easiest method of access will vary from brand to brand.

Oil on race

Oil on edge of hook

Access from under needle plate

The rattle from the hook area is the indicator that oil is required. If the machine has a stitch counter that prompts you to oil, remember to reset it, as per the manual.

METAL DROP-IN BOBBIN

There is plenty of metal-on-metal movement in this sewing system, and the hook should be oiled every 8–12 hours of actual sewing time.

Oiling metal drop-in bobbin hook area

Another style of metal drop-in bobbin

LARGE VERTICAL ROTARY HOOK

This style of sewing machine has a small reservoir under the needle plate. A wicking system transports oil to the edge of the hook. The reservoir gives a longer lasting supply of oil to the hook, so the frequency of oiling is somewhat less on these machines. They also have a stitch counter that reminds you when to oil. The machine does not know if it has been oiled, so you need to follow the instructions to reset the counter. The manufacturer provides a tube of special oil with these models. When you run out of it, be sure to replace it with the same type. Follow the manufacturers' specifications on how many drops to place in the reservoir.

Also, two spots inside the hook have wicks. One drop on each is sufficient.

Oiling reservoir; note red indicator.

Oil wicks in hook

REAR-FACING LARGE VERTICAL HOOK

To oil this hook, open the bobbin door and the hook will swing forward. Turn the handwheel backward until the hook is in the position shown in the photo. One drop is sufficient. Do not over-oil. These machines also use a special oil provided by the manufacturer. Be sure to replace with the same oil when you run out.

Proper oiling position

PLASTIC DROP-IN BOBBIN

Some of these machines have a wick in the center of the hook. This is visible when you take out the bobbin case. *Remember: This is a wick, not lint!* I have seen these removed by people when cleaning the bobbin area.

I occasionally oil the spot where the plastic bobbin case meets the metal part of the hook, though there is some debate about doing this. I oil it only when I feel it is noisy. The important thing to remember is to use a very tiny drop of oil.

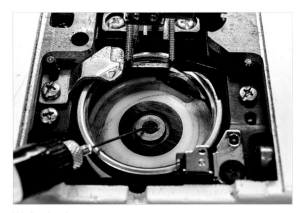

Wick in hook

Oil where bobbin case meets hook.

FLOATING ROTARY HOOK

For this system, you can put a small drop of oil on the edge of the hook to lessen noise coming from the area.

Oiling location

Summary

Any time you put oil in the hook area of your sewing machine, it is a good practice to stitch on some scrap fabric. This gets rid of excess oil and keeps it off your project. The hook-bobbin case area can be a source of high wear on a sewing machine. Regular lubrication will not only dramatically increase the life of your machine but also make your experience more pleasant by keeping noise at a minimum.

Oiling the Upper Portion of the Machine

After you have opened the top part of the machine to the degree that you are comfortable with and have cleaned, you can also lubricate. Oil should be used sparingly, one drop at each location. Make sure you are using an appropriate sewing machine oil. Refer to your sewing machine manual for where to oil.

A word of caution: I do not recommend opening past the take-up area on computerized sewing machines.

Circuitry under the top and front covers is susceptible to static electricity. The opening and lubrication of these machines should be left to qualified sewing machine technicians. I recommend caution even opening the take-up area on these machines. Make sure the power is off and turn the wheel by hand.

TAKE-UP AREA

Many sewing machines give you access to the thread take-up area. Sometimes you only need to open a door. For others, you might need to take out a screw. The linkages of that mechanism usually have small oil ports to help guide you to the right spots.

Oil ports

Turning the handwheel and watching the action will let you see the moving linkage that needs oil. Keep a lookout for caught threads.

TOP MAIN SHAFT AREA

If you have a machine where the top cover is easily removed and you are comfortable with removing it, then you can also put a drop of oil in the right spots. Usually removing a couple of screws gives you access to the insides. Some machines have hinged top covers, which provide easy access to oil ports.

Oil where you see metal parts moving on metal. Turning the handwheel makes it easy to see where that is happening. My advice is to unplug the sewing machine before you do this. Many manuals will have oiling guides in them.

Typical oiling spots in mechanical machine

Summary

Use oil sparingly. It is better to oil less and more often. These instructions should be seen as light maintenance. Even if you oil regularly, take the machine to a qualified sewing machine technician for regular, thorough service.

TIP If a sewing machine sits idle for a length of time, some oils may start to gel. This makes the machine hard to turn. It is a good idea to run a machine now and then, even if you are not going to sew. This keeps things turning smoothly, and it will be ready for you when you want to sew. If you have let your sewing machine sit for a very long time, it might be advisable to give it a light oiling before you start to sew. This replaces oil that might have evaporated and dilutes any residue left behind.

OTHER MAINTENANCE

Firmware Updates

Many of today's higher-end computerized sewing machines use firmware to run them. These are just like the operating systems on your computers. One of the great things about firmware is that it can be changed. Manufacturers may find that something wasn't programmed optimally when the machine first went to market. They might want to add a feature or stitches. Firmware can be reprogrammed to deal with these things.

Usually you can download the new version from the manufacturer's website and load it onto the sewing machine yourself. If you are not comfortable with that, most dealers would be happy to do it for you. It is worth it to check with your dealer or the brand's website to stay informed of changes. That way your machine always stays current.

Mechanical Updates

The consumer demand for new features, combined with brand competitiveness, means that new machines are hitting the market faster than ever before. This means not only new firmware but also new mechanical designs. It is often the case that after a new machine comes out, the manufacturer changes a mechanical part. This may be due a flaw or possibly just that they have found a better one. It is important to stay informed about these updates. The dealer will receive notification from the manufacturer, and it is a good idea to ask about this occasionally during the warranty period.

MAGNETS AND COMPUTERIZED SEWING MACHINES

I am frequently asked if it is all right to use magnetic pincushions and other types of magnets near computerized sewing machines. I can honestly say that I have never seen one affected. I have seen phones and other products that use chips damaged though. I recommend erring on the side of caution, and unless the manufacturer states it is okay, I would avoid keeping magnets too close.

Surge Protectors

It is wise to protect your expensive computerized machine with a surge protector. Most power bars do not offer real protection, so make sure that what you are using can stop a spike in electricity from destroying your circuitry. Your local electronics shop will be able to advise you as to the best option. A power conditioner is probably not necessary, as your computerized sewing machine already converts the 110V alternating current to DC power.

A Few Other Things

Going Over Heavy Seams (Climbing Seams)

Going over heavy seams can be a challenge. You can set yourself up for success by following a few steps.

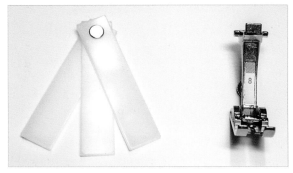

Tools for climbing seams: height compensation tool and jeans foot

• Lower the presser foot pressure. That will help the foot rise up and over.

• Use specialty feet if they are available for your machine. Some machines have a jeans foot that works very well.

• Increase the stitch length.

• Flatten the seam with a wooden clapper or rubber mallet before stitching.

• Use a stronger but not necessarily thicker needle, such as the HLx5 Hard Chrome Needle (by Organ Needle Company, page 104).

• Use a shim under the presser foot to compensate for the height difference.

Using Spray Baste and Fusible Stabilizers

These products were created to help make some sewing tasks easier. Some of them can create problems for you, however. It is important to make sure that the product was designed to be used with a sewing machine.

Very sticky glues can interfere with proper stitch formation. The thread is prevented from forming the right-size loop behind the needle (see How a Stitch Is Formed, page 10), and your machine may start skipping stitches and breaking thread. If you see a ring of glue form around the needle, this is often a clue.

If you are experiencing either of these problems and you have just started using a product that involves glue, you may have to switch to a lighter version.

When you are using a product with glue, check the area under the needle plate and the feed dogs (as shown at right). You might find a buildup there. This will need to be removed.

Glue in feed dogs

Turning the Handwheel

This might seem an odd subject, but it is surprising how many times I run across problems that are created by bringing this old habit to a new sewing machine.

If you have switched from a mechanical sewing machine to one that has an automatic needle stop, it is very likely that for a while you will still reach for the handwheel at the end of a seam. It's a habit you develop with older sewing machines that just stop randomly in any part of their stitching cycle—you turn the wheel to bring the needle out and remove the fabric.

Most newer machines have a choice of where the needle stops, either down in the fabric or in its up position. These stops are programmed to be in their optimal resting spot. The down stop is positioned to allow you to pivot the fabric or just let you stop and inspect without the fabric shifting. The up stop is designed to allow you to start sewing without having a tangle on the back of your fabric.

If you chose the stop down position, it is important to use the electronic method your machine provides to bring the needle back up. This could be a button, a press on the foot control, or a choice of either. Doing this takes the needle to exactly the right position. You can then start sewing your next seam without creating a thread nest and having the spool of thread suddenly flying off the spool pin. The eye of the needle will also be in just the right spot for the needle threader to work (see Machine Needle Threaders, page 111).

If you prefer to move the needle manually, then turn the handwheel *toward* you until the needle just barely starts its downward path after reaching the top. The best advice though is to enjoy the feature that you paid for.

One consequence of starting to sew with the needle in the wrong position is the potential for a thread lock (see Thread Lock, page 97).

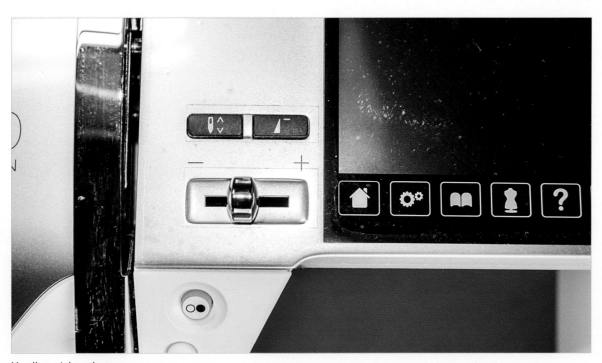

Needle-up-/-down button

PROBLEMS AND HOW TO FIX THEM

Relationship problems often arise because of communication issues. I see the same thing with sewing machine troubles. When you are frustrated because your thread is looping or you are unable to climb a seam, what is your machine trying to tell you? What can you do to help it successfully achieve the task at hand?

TENSION IN THE RELATIONSHIP

Bad tension can ruin any relationship. You are trying to sew a simple seam and are getting a nest of thread under the fabric. You might be using two colors of thread, and you are seeing the bobbin thread being pulled to the top of the fabric. Last week, when you were working on this project, the tension was perfect. What is your machine trying to tell you today?

Your expectations are not being met, and that is frustrating. The key is knowing what you are dealing with. Is the machine misbehaving, or is this simply a misunderstanding?

Let's explore how tension mechanisms work.

Top Tension

The top tension mechanism is actually a very simple thing. It really doesn't want to give you any grief, and it rarely does.

Basically, two metal discs provide the tension on the top thread. On one side, a spring regulates the amount of pressure to the thread. In the photo, I am using two pie plates to symbolize the metal discs. My hand on one side represents the spring. The harder I push, the more tension there is.

That spring is controlled by a dial or, in the case of some computerized sewing machines, by the computer itself. Increasing the number increases the amount of pressure on the thread. Decreasing the number lessens the amount of pressure on the thread. The control dial can be found on top of the machine on some brands and on the front of the machine on others. On older machines, you might find the dial on the left side. On machines where the tension is controlled by the computer, there will be an icon on screen that allows adjustment when touched. Your instruction manual will indicate where the tension control is for your machine.

Tension discs

Dial on top of machine

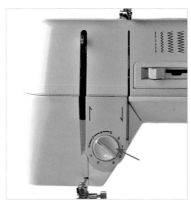

Dial on front of machine

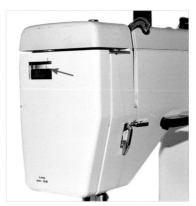

Dial on side of machine

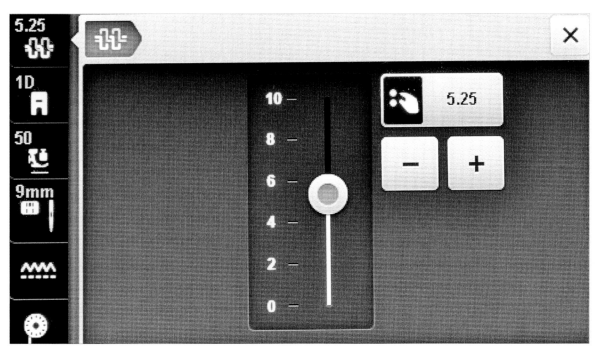

Icon on screen

How the Presser Foot Is Involved

When you raise the presser foot, the discs separate and allow the top thread to slip all the way between them.

As you lower the foot to sew, the discs come together and provide the selected amount of pressure to the thread.

Open discs; thread slips in between.

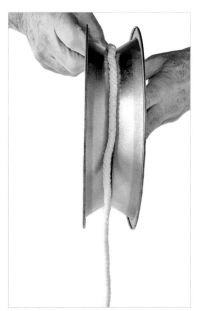

Closed discs; thread stays outside.

If you thread your machine with the presser foot down, the top thread does not enter the discs and therefore has no tension. The result will be that the top thread is pulled to the back of the fabric, sometimes in long loops.

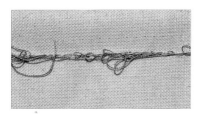

Loops of top thread on back of fabric

Setting the Top Tension

Top tension has many increments of adjustment. Manufacturers usually give a range of 0–9. Don't let this intimidate you! I have had many sewists tell me that an instructor has frightened them by yelling, "Never touch your tension!" intimating that something bad may happen if you touch that dial. Nothing could be further from the truth. Your machine will not explode. In this relationship, you are in charge! You just have to know what to communicate to your machine.

There is a reason the adjustment is there, and when you understand how simple the principal is, you and your sewing machine will sing a harmonious duet!

The higher the number you select, the tighter the tension on the top thread. The lower the number, the lower the tension.

Tension dial with adjustment range of 0–9

TIP Many machines have two sets of tension discs. A metal divider in between gives another path for the thread. These are provided for situations when you use two top threads, such as pin tucking. For normal use with one thread, it doesn't matter which side of the divider you put the thread into.

Bottom (Bobbin) Tension

The bobbin tension provides the yang to the top tension's yin. When the two are balanced, the stitch looks great and the fabric is held together firmly and without puckers or loops.

Two different styles of bobbin tension mechanism

Over the years, manufacturers have created their own ways to form a stitch, and it's in the bobbin area that you will find the most variation. Although there are many styles of bobbin cases, for the most part, the adjustment is accomplished the same way. They have a screw that is tightened for more tension and loosened for less. For photos of the different bobbin cases, see Sewing Systems and Hook Types (page 11) to determine which type you have.

Threading the Tension Spring

Most bobbin cases have a tension spring that needs to be threaded. On some, a lever pushes down on the top of the bobbin to create tension.

In the horizontal drop-in-bobbin-type bobbin case, it is a very common occurrence to forget to pull the thread into the tension spring.

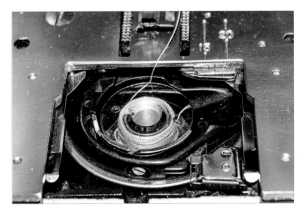

Incorrectly threaded

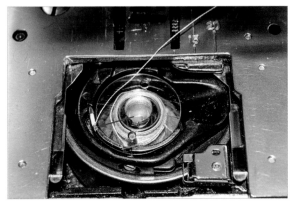

Correctly threaded

Here is how the stitching looks when the thread is not in the tension spring and the bobbin thread is pulled to the top.

In the vertical type of removable bobbin case, it seems to happen less frequently, possibly because the case is removed to load the bobbin.

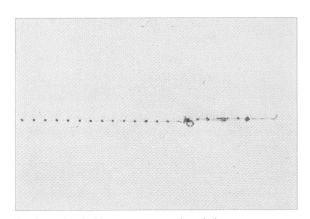

Stitching when bobbin tension is not threaded

Correctly threaded removable bobbin case

The final authority on threading the bobbin case for your model of machine is, of course, your manual.

Using the Right Bobbin

A common cause of problems is using the wrong bobbins for your type of sewing system. Many bobbins look the same or have very slight variations. However, using the wrong one can cause not only tension problems but breaking thread. A good policy is to buy the same bobbin that came with the machine originally.

In the example below, notice that the bobbin in the machine is slightly higher than the top edge of the bobbin case. As the top thread tries to come over the top to form a knot, it catches under the bobbin and jams the machine. At a minimum, this is frustrating, but there is also a chance it will end up spinning the bobbin case around and damaging it.

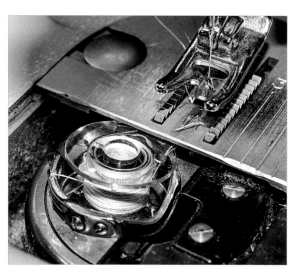

Incorrect drop-in bobbin

In the following example, the bobbin is too narrow and will move around, creating the possibility of the needle hitting it and causing damage.

Incorrect vertical bobbin

TIP **Prewound Bobbins**

Prewound bobbins work well, provided they match the size of the bobbin meant for the sewing machine. However, if the machine has a low-bobbin warning, it will most likely not work when you use these bobbins.

Tension Calibration and Adjustment

Now that you have a better understanding of the tension mechanisms involved, take control and make your stitch look like it should. This is really a very simple procedure, and when you're done, you should never be afraid of tension again.

Finding the Default Top Tension

Every machine has a default setting for top tension. The easiest are the computerized versions. When you turn on the machine, it automatically goes to the right setting for the stitch, in this case straight stitch. These machines typically have touch screens, but some don't. On those you may see the dial move on start-up.

Some manufacturers designate a position for the dial labeled Auto. This is the setting you want for those machines.

Some machines have a mark on the dial that designates the default setting.

Auto tension

Mark on dial

For the machines with a few numbers highlighted on the dial, select the middle number.

Most other machines will have a dial with a range of adjustment from 0 to 9. On those, you will select 4.5.

Dial from 0 to 9

Making and Analyzing a Sample

Very little can ever go wrong with the top tension mechanism, other than something getting stuck between the discs. That is why you are going to trust these numbers, having made sure, of course, that the discs are clear. Before you start, make sure that the top tension is set to default (see Finding the Default Top Tension, page 73). There is a chance that the default setting is not correct on your machine, but this is not a common problem. If it is, you need to take it in to your sewing machine technician and have it set properly. This calibration process assumes that yours is right.

1. Thread the machine with a good quality 50/2-weight light-colored thread, such as Aurifil or DMC.

2. Use the same thread in the bobbin. *Do not miss this important step!* You want to work with a very

light-colored thread. The reason for this will become evident shortly.

3. Insert a brand new sharps 80/12 needle. A new needle means one out of the package, not from the pincushion.

4. Using a piece of good quality cotton in a very light color (such as Kona Snow or equivalent), fold the fabric so you will be sewing on two layers.

5. Set the stitch length at 2.5 or as close as your machine will allow and sew a straight stitch 4˝–5˝ long.

6. When you are done, inspect the stitching by looking in the hole created by the needle. The knot made by the top and bottom thread should be in there. Use a magnifying glass if necessary.

Look at both the top and bottom of the fabric. The knot should be right in the middle. To make it easier to see, the following photo uses a prop to show the location of the knot in the fabric.

Prop showing knot in middle of fabric

You may find that this is not the case and that the knot is more to one side of the fabric than the other.

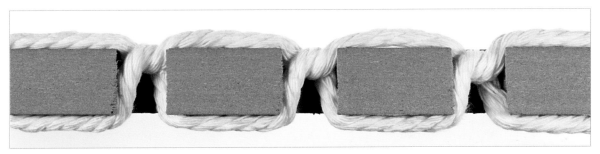

Knot pulled to the top

Knot pulled to the bottom

Making Adjustments

If your knot is not centered perfectly, then you will need to adjust the bobbin tension. Have no fear, you won't mess anything up.

In Styles of Bobbin Case (page 21), you saw the different types of bobbin cases and adjustment screws. The adjustment screw is what you need to turn. The direction depends on what the sample stitch out showed you.

If the knot is pulled to the top of the fabric, tighten the screw. If the knot is pulled toward the underside of the fabric, loosen the screw.

Remember: Righty tighty, lefty loosey.

Righty tighty, lefty loosey

Make the increment of adjustment very small, maybe a quarter of a turn. Sew another seam and examine it again. Adjust until you have centered the knot perfectly.

Congratulations! You have just taken control of a very important aspect of this relationship.

What Could Go Wrong?

Now that you are feeling powerful, try a simple exercise: Unthread the machine and take out the bobbin. Rethread the machine with the same type of thread, only in black. Remember to wind some of this black thread onto the bobbin as well.

Sew another seam right beside the best one you did after calibration. I'm guessing that you are not going to be as happy with this row of stitching as you are with the one beside it.

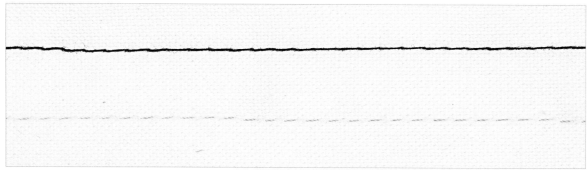

Row of dark stitching

Now take a black piece of cotton fabric and fold it in half. Fold it over the bottom of the light-colored fabric.

Start sewing a seam on the light fabric and continue onto the black. Examine the stitching. The tension seems to change as you transition from one color to the next, but the machine doesn't know what fabric you are on. As you sew onto the black, the tension looks good again.

Stitching on two colors

Your calibration is good, and the tension is right. The problem with the stitching on the light-colored fabric is simply the color contrast with the thread. Dark threads on light fabrics do not stitch out well. You might be convinced that you have a tension problem when you really don't.

The reason for this exercise is to explain that whenever the stitching is going to show, it is a good idea to test-sew. Topstitching, machine quilting, and buttonholes are good examples where you may want to limit how much contrast there is between thread and fabric. Interestingly, using light thread on dark fabric does not create as bad a look.

Things That Might Affect Tension

Your tension should now be calibrated. This is something that you might have to do occasionally. The adjustment screws on the bobbin case can loosen with the vibration of the sewing machine.

For this exercise, you used good thread and used it top and bottom. That may not always be the case when you are sewing.

• You may choose to use different threads made of different fibers.

• There might be times when you want to use different weights of thread on top and bottom.

• Decorative threads have very different properties from those you used in our calibration.

These things will all change how the stitching looks. Now that you have set up the machine properly, you will not have to adjust the bobbin tension. All adjustments will be made from the top.

Situations That Might Require Top Tension Adjustment

Heavier thread on top A heavier thread is usually less supple than a lighter one.

Monofilament or other plastic threads These threads, either round or flat, create extra tension wherever they contact metal. This means the tension discs and all thread guides, as well as the needle.

Different brands of the same weight thread Even different brands can behave differently. Some threads have more sizing in them and are less supple. Some are just lesser quality and are not as smooth and even.

Different colors top and bottom Sometimes you might want to use a different color from the top thread in the bobbin. In this case, depending on the thickness of the fabric, when you look in the needle hole, you might see the thread from the opposite side show through.

In all these situations, you can balance the tension properly by using your upper tension control.

Making Top Tension Adjustments

With the top tension control, you can very precisely control the position of the knot in the fabric.

Knot in middle—proper tension adjustment

When the knot is pulled too far down in the fabric, increase the top tension by setting it to a higher number. *Raise the number, raise the knot.*

Knot toward bottom and needs to be raised

When the knot is pulled toward the top of the fabric, decrease the top tension by lowering the number. *Lower the number, lower the knot.*

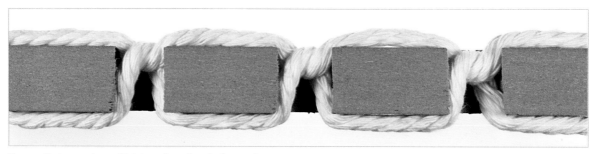

Knot pulled toward top of fabric and needs to be lowered

Controlling the tension is really that easy. When your machine is calibrated properly, you raise and lower only the top tension number to move the knot to where you want it.

This knowledge gives you the freedom to play with different threads with confidence. You can achieve the kind of results you want.

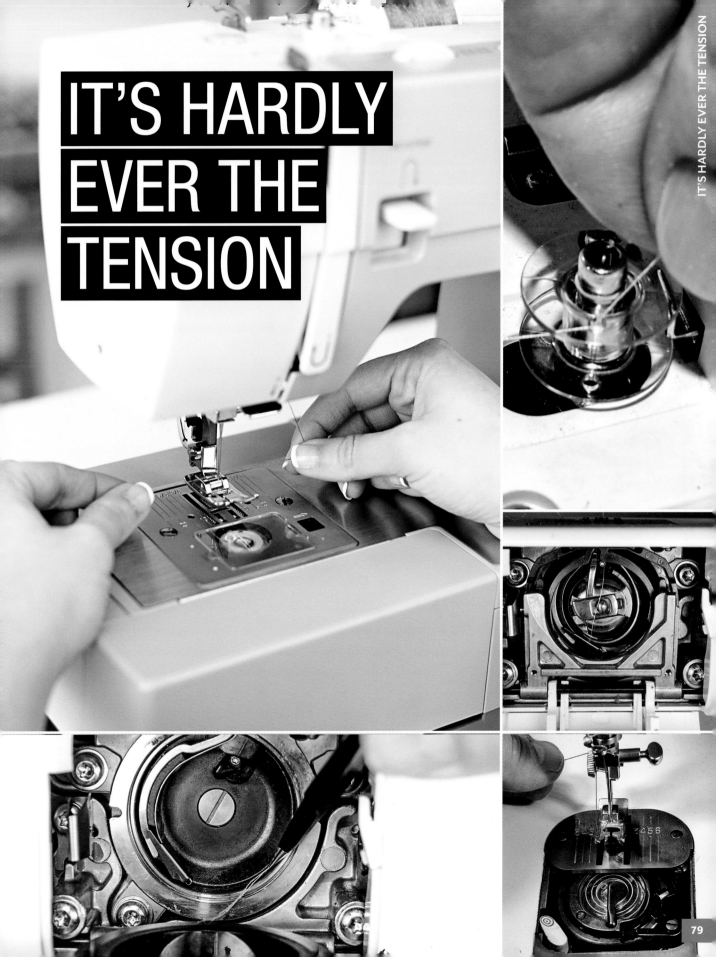

IT'S HARDLY EVER THE TENSION

Most often what looks like a tension problem actually isn't. As important as it is to know how and when to adjust, it is just as or more important to be able to recognize and fix a problem that disguises itself as tension. Most of the other problems are very simple, as you will see in this chapter.

Smoothing Burrs on the Hook

Refer to Sewing Systems and Hook Types (page 11).

The hook is the metal part that revolves around the bobbin case. It is responsible for picking the thread up from the back of the needle and pulling it over top of the bobbin to form a knot with the bobbin thread.

 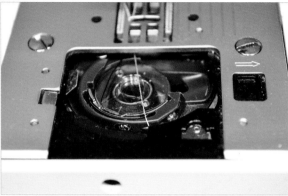

Top thread being pulled over bobbin by hook

If the hook has a rough spot on it, particularly on the tip, the top thread will not be pulled around smoothly. This may show up as uneven tension, loops under the fabric, or even breaking thread. Your first thought may be, *I need to adjust the tension.*

These rough spots or *burrs* are caused by breaking needles or even by deflecting needles coming in contact with the tip of the hook.

Let's take a look at each of these systems individually and see where to look for the burrs.

Oscillating or CB hook   In the photo below, an arrow points at the tip of the hook. This is often where you will find a burr. They are almost never on the front or flat side, but rather on the sloped part. The best way to find the burr is to slide your fingernail toward the tip and feel for the roughness.

Another arrow points at the second spot where you might find needle damage. This should be more visible. It happens when the needle deflects while in the fabric and makes direct contact. This type of hook also had a plastic version that can have needle damage on the black portion.

Oscillating hook with plastic variant

Industrial-style rotary hook   One arrow points at the tip of the hook. Run your fingernail toward the tip on the sloped side. This is where you will find the burr. The second arrow points at a flat piece of metal called the *bail*. If you run your nail along the outer edge of this bail, you might well find rough spots where a deflecting needle has made contact.

Drop-in bobbin horizontal rotary hook   The arrow is pointing at the tip of the hook. Slide your fingernail along the sloped part toward and off the end of the tip to find a burr. Feel around the top inside edge for rough spots as well.

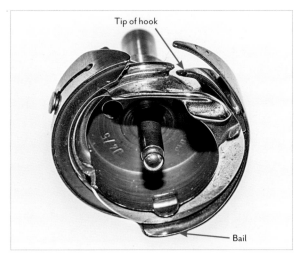

Industrial-style rotary hook

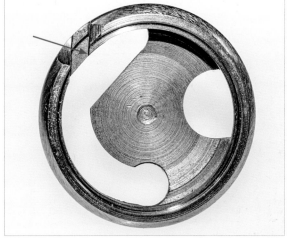

Drop-in bobbin horizontal rotary hook

Large vertical rotary hook   The tip of the hook is marked by the arrow. Run your fingernail down the sloped part off the end to find a burr.

Floating vertical rotary hook   The arrow points at the tip of the hook. Run your fingernail along the sloped part off the end to find a burr. With this type of hook, make sure to examine the plastic portion for any needle damage.

Large vertical rotary hook

Floating vertical rotary hook

High-speed rear-facing large vertical rotary hook
This hook swings forward when you open the bobbin door. You won't be able to remove it to check for burrs. Your technician will have to check this when the machine is in for service.

After you have determined if there is a burr or any other damage from needle strikes, you can use a piece of 400-grit (a.k.a. #400) wet and dry sandpaper and polish off any roughness. The #400 is smooth enough that you will not scratch the metal or plastic parts. The large high-speed rear-facing vertical rotary hook is the only one that I would recommend you do not polish. I suggest you take it to your dealer if you find needle damage. Never polish the flat edge of the hook tip. Work only on the part that slopes toward the tip.

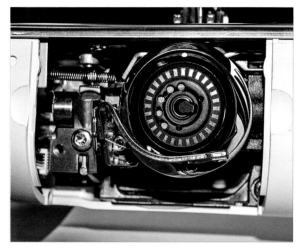

High-speed rear-facing large vertical rotary hook

Thread

Thread quality, thickness, and number of plies are often overlooked when analyzing stitch quality. It is one of those important variables. Different threads labeled as the same weight may not look the same when sewn, due simply to the manufacturing process. If your stitching does not meet your standard, maybe you have changed brands recently. You may need to alter the tension to compensate (see Top Tension, page 68).

Damage to the Bobbin Case

Refer to Sewing Systems and Hook Types (page 11).

Oscillating or CB   This type of bobbin case rarely sustains any damage. It can, however, become tarnished with time. When that happens, you may start to hear a slight snapping sound when the top thread passes over it. The stitching may also start looking bad with small loops underneath. The thread may start to break. The solution is to shine up the bobbin case with a metal polish. After the luster is restored, it will function

Tarnished oscillating or CB bobbin case

properly again. The best and easiest to use product I have found for this is The Original Never-Dull Magic Wadding Polish (by The George Basch Company). It is a wadding with the chemical infused and does a great job.

Industrial-style bobbin case These bobbin cases seem more prone to needle strikes and should be examined for needle marks. These can be polished with #400 wet and dry sandpaper. Those needle strikes, as well as dropping the bobbin case on a hard floor, can also cause them to go out of round. If you are pulling on the bobbin thread and you can feel a tight spot every revolution, this has probably happened. I have had good success reshaping, using needle-nose pliers. Gently pull the metal back to round. This style of bobbin case can also benefit from a polishing if it is tarnished.

Caution: It is possible to break the metal, so this is something you might want to leave to your sewing machine technician.

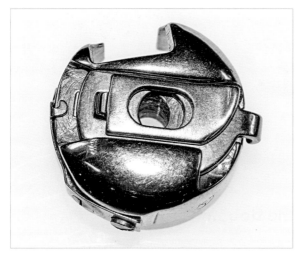

Industrial-style bobbin case

Reshaping with needle-nose pliers

Drop-in bobbin case These are the most susceptible to damage from the needle, but they can be repaired with a good degree of success. Often, usually as a result of incorrect threading or using too heavy a thread, top thread can wrap around and spin these bobbin cases into the path of the needle. This creates rough needle holes that then catch the top thread in its path around the bobbin. Scratches around the edges and underneath can also result. Using #400 wet and dry sandpaper, you can polish out most of the rough spots. Sometimes, if there is too much damage, you may have to replace this bobbin case.

Drop-in bobbin case showing damage

Large vertical rotary bobbin case   These bobbin cases don't often suffer trauma from the needle. It is a good idea to check the position of the wire loop, as they can be dislodged occasionally. If so, it is best to have your sewing machine technician repair it.

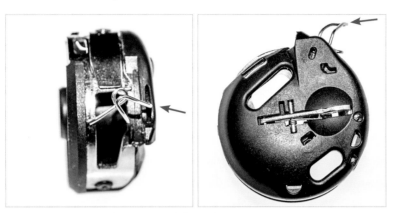
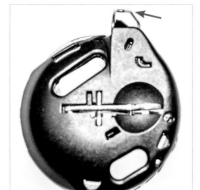

Large vertical rotary bobbin case with dislodged wire loop

Wire loop in correct position

High-speed rear-facing vertical bobbin case   Keeping this area free of stray thread is important. A tool provided by the manufacturer can be inserted into the gap between bobbin case and hook to clear caught threads.

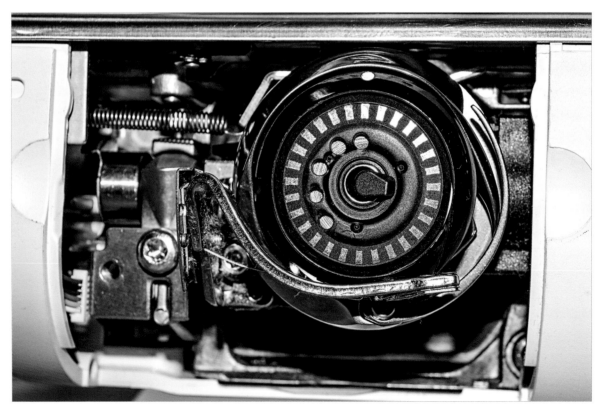

Large vertical rear-facing bobbin case

Incorrect Threading

Threading is often overlooked as a source of tension problems, and it is most often the cause. While most machines work on the same threading principals, there are slight variations from brand to brand.

Presser Foot Up

One of the major causes of problems is not lifting the presser foot before threading. This action opens up the tension discs and allows the top thread to slide between. When the foot is dropped, the discs close on the thread and create tension. The main symptom is loops on the back of the fabric.

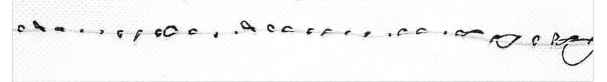

Loops caused by threading with foot down

Missing the Take-Up Lever

It is possible to miss threading the take-up lever that moves up and down on the front of most machines. When this happens, the thread will tangle around the bobbin case in long loops. In some cases, it will spin the plastic drop-in bobbin cases around and possibly create needle damage that will need to be polished out. Sometimes the damage will be too great, and the bobbin case will need to be replaced.

Some machines have a hidden take-up lever. This calls for a little extra care when threading. If the machine is computerized, take one stitch with the foot control before threading. This positions the lever and the needle in the right place for proper threading.

If the machine is mechanical, with no automatic needle stop, turn the handwheel toward you until the needle has just started on its downward path. This should position everything properly.

Take-up lever

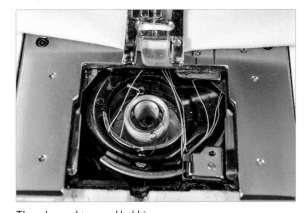

Threads caught around bobbin case

Skipping a Thread Guide

The thread guides on your sewing machine serve the important function of ensuring the thread is following its intended path. Missing a guide can be the cause of what looks like a tension problem. Always thread all guides, including the one directly above the needle.

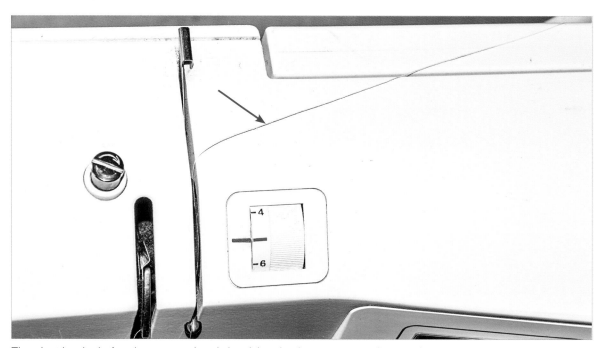

Thread guide at back of machine was not threaded, and thread is about to pop out of tension discs.

Guide above needle not threaded; stitch quality may suffer.

Wrong Size of Thread Stopper

If you use the horizontal spool pin on your machine, it is important that you use the proper size stopper. If it's too large for the spool of thread, it can cause the thread to catch as it unwinds close to the stopper. If it's too small for the spool, it can cause the thread to catch on notches and imperfections on the edge of the spool itself.

Stopper too large

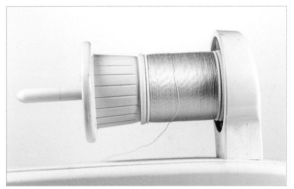

Correct size

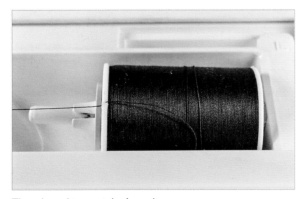

Stopper too small

Correct size

Thread caught on notch of spool

It is also very important that you inspect the outer edge of the stopper for nicks and places for the tread to catch. If possible, polish them smooth with #400 wet and dry sandpaper.

Needle Plate Damage

A very common cause of perceived tension problems is needle damage to the needle plate. As the needle enters the slot or hole in the plate, as well as when it is on its way back up, the top thread can get caught on one of the sharp notches. This can cause bad stitching and breaking thread.

The rough spots on the inside of the opening can be polished with fine abrasive cord. The damage on the surface can be polished with #400 wet and dry sandpaper.

In some cases, the plate will be damaged beyond repair and should be replaced. Never grind out the plate to repair it. The hollow created can cause the fabric to move up and down as the needle goes in and out. This is called *flagging* and can cause skipped stitches on some finer fabrics.

Damaged needle plate

Repaired needle plate

Spool Pin Orientation

Most sewing machines have two spool pins. With some, the extra one will be in the accessories box. Often one of these will be horizontal and the other vertical. The spool pin you choose to use can also make a difference to your stitch quality.

Horizontal Spool Pin

The horizontal spool pin does not allow your spool of thread to spin. This causes the thread to twist. This twisting can show up in your stitching here and there as a slanted stitch. With some threads, the twisting can be so bad that the thread creates a loop that can get caught in a guide and catch or break the thread. The benefit of this spool pin is that it is quiet because the spool does not spin. The advantages and disadvantages will need to be weighed by each sewist.

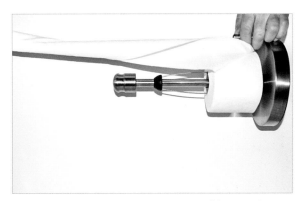

Prop showing how thread twists as it comes off horizontal spool pin

Vertical Spool Pin

The vertical spool pin allows the spool of thread to turn as it unwinds. This prevents the thread from twisting, delivering a more consistent stitch. The disadvantage is that it is noisier because the spool is turning.

> **NOTE** *It is important to note that if you are using one of the larger spools of thread, such as the popular 1,300-meter variety, they are heavier, and you might have to turn down the top tension slightly until it is about half full. This is to compensate for the extra tension created by the weight of the thread itself. It is a good idea to have a spool pin felt under the thread to reduce friction.*

Prop showing how thread doesn't twist as it comes off vertical spool pin

TIP The black stuff that you see on the vertical spool pin is glue from the label on the thread. This glue is very sticky and can stop the spool from turning freely. It is a good idea to clean it off with a tissue and some rubbing alcohol. This will help keep stitch quality consistent.

Vertical spool pin covered with glue

Independent Thread Stand

These stand-alone thread stands can be used for large cones of thread that don't fit onto the sewing machine. Even though they have a vertical spool pin, it is important to note that, because the thread goes first to a guide above the cone, the cone does not turn. This means that the thread will twist.

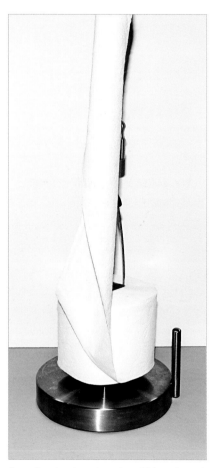

Prop showing thread coming off thread stand

Parallel-Wound versus Cross-Wound Thread

Both types of thread work well. The reason I mention them is the belief that the cross-wound thread will work better on the horizontal spool pin. While it does work better than the parallel-wound spools, it still twists as it comes off. This is particularly true when the spool is closer to empty. Metallic threads and monofilaments will twist badly.

Parallel-wound thread

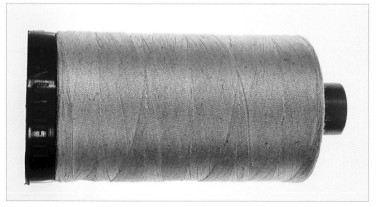

Cross-wound thread with twists

If possible, it is wise to use the vertical spool pin to deliver the top thread. This will improve stitch quality due to less twist in the thread.

Bobbins

Loosely Wound Bobbins

A loosely wound bobbin will give less than perfect results.

Loosely wound bobbin

Properly wound bobbin

The important key to getting a bobbin wound properly is to use the pre-tension as specified by the manufacturer. This gives the thread exactly the right amount of pressure needed to wind evenly and tightly. There are many variations and placements of this mechanism, and to get it right, you will need to refer to the manual for your model. Here are a few:

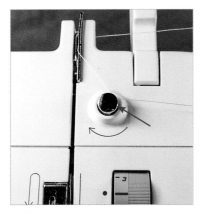

Bobbin-winder pre-tension

It is a good idea to refer to your manual to ensure that you are using all the required thread guides when winding a bobbin.

Overfilled Bobbins

Even a slightly overfilled bobbin can get stuck in the bobbin case and add extra tension. Most sewing machines have an adjustable bobbin stop. They are easy to adjust and can make the difference between good and bad stitching with a newly filled bobbin.

The stop should be adjusted so the machine stops winding just before the thread reaches the edge of the bobbin. The adjustment screw should be barely loosened, and the stop can be moved to the desired position. *Do not loosen the screw too far* or you may undo a nut underneath that could fall into the sewing machine.

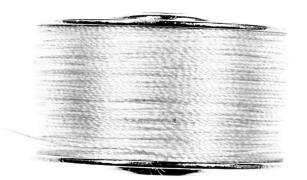

Properly filled

Overfilled

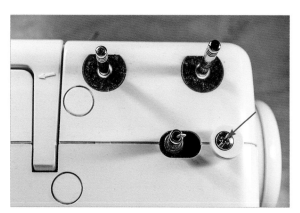

Adjustment screw

Adjustment screw

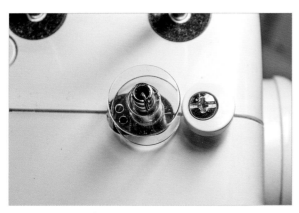

This will allow overfilling.

Correctly set adjustable bobbin stop

There are many variations for the placement of the adjustment screw, but it will always be beside the winder mechanism.

Some machines do not have an external adjustment. These will need to be taken in to see the sewing machine technician if a change is required.

It is worth noting: A bobbin that has been wound with more thread on one side than the other may not cause a tension problem, but it will not allow you to fill it to its capacity.

Bobbin with more thread on one side

That Extra Little Piece of Thread

An uneven bobbin tension can be caused by that little tail of stray thread that can be present after winding a bobbin.

Bobbin with extra tail of thread

When you insert the bobbin into its bobbin case, that piece of thread often ends up caught between the edge of the bobbin and the inside of the bobbin case. This will cause what looks like a tension issue.

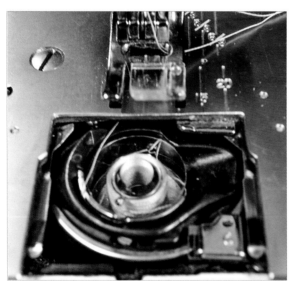

Thread caught between bobbin and bobbin case (horizontal system)

Thread caught between bobbin and bobbin case (vertical system)

You can do two things to solve the problem: Either cut off the little piece of thread very close to the bobbin or wind it slightly differently.

To wind without a tail, put the thread through the hole in the side of the bobbin, from the inside to the outside. Hang onto this thread as you are winding. If you hold it close to the bobbin and don't let go, it should break off on its own.

Some machines have bobbins that have a rough post inside. These you only need to wrap a few times and then cut off on the cutter built into the bobbin-winder engagement lever.

Put thread through hole in side of bobbin and hold tail.

Wrap thread around bobbin and cut.

Some brands have a slot underneath the bobbin that holds the thread in place after cutting.

Wrap thread around bobbin and cut.

Machines with Self-Winding Bobbins

Many sewing machines have self-winding bobbin systems. They allow you to wind without removing the bobbin from the bobbin case. The key to proper winding is to secure the top thread around the presser-foot screw and have the activation lever, or in some cases the bobbin-cover slide plate, in the right position. Some models have a friction ring around the presser-foot screw that will hold the thread for you. Some you will need to hold until the thread breaks off at the bobbin.

Move activating lever to the left and hold onto thread until it has broken off.

Move activating lever to the right. Thread is held in friction ring.

In another version, line up the triangles on the slide plate and slip the top thread into the friction ring on the presser foot screw (as shown by the arrow in the top right photo).

As always, refer to your manual to get the best results for your model.

Damaged Bobbins

Even sewing machine technicians, when trying to hunt down a tension problem, can overlook damaged bobbins. I have seen chipped, bent, and even broken bobbins in machines. Bobbins for the most part are inexpensive and should be replaced when damaged.

Chipped bobbin

Bent bobbin

Broken bobbin

Thread Lock

A sewing machine can be easily stopped in its tracks by a thread lock. A piece of thread gets caught in the hook and completely jams the machine. This happens with all styles of sewing systems (see Sewing Systems and Hook Types, page 11). The reason is usually that the needle and take-up lever were not in the right position when the seam was started.

If you have an oscillating- or CB-hook or removable rotary hook machine, simply open the race gate and pull out the hook. The thread can then be easily removed.

If the machine is rotary, turn the handwheel slowly backward with increasing pressure until the thread breaks loose. Try to find and remove the culprit. If you feel that too much force is called for, then you should take the machine to the sewing machine technician.

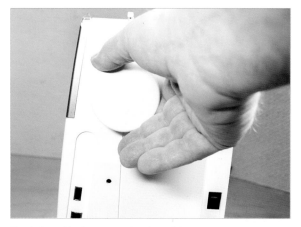

Removing thread lock, oscillating hook

Break thread lock on rotary hook machine

For the drop-in bobbin systems, remove the threads wrapped around the bobbin case, making sure that it has not popped out of position.

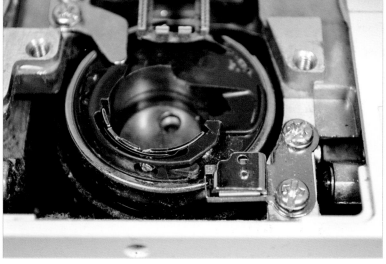

Proper drop-in bobbin case position

NEEDLES, THREADERS, AND AUTOMATIC THREAD CUTTERS

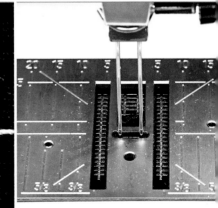

Needles

Next to the tension, needles are probably the most misunderstood part of the sewing machine and yet one of the most important. This is quite understandable. As fabric and thread choices have increased, needle manufacturers have come up with adaptations and design features to deal with them.

When I started in this industry, there were fewer choices, and it was simple to choose the right needle for the job. Now when you go into a store, a whole wall full of different styles and sizes can boggle the mind. In this chapter, we will try to demystify and simplify the choices.

Anatomy of a Needle

The least expensive sewing notion you will buy for your projects is going to be the sewing machine needle. The right needle is an unsung hero quietly going about its work without drama. The wrong needle is devious and stealthy, causing problems and making you think it's your machine or worse ... you. For many, needles, and why there are so many different types, are a complete mystery.

Note: The following photos use props to show needles, thread, and fabric.

A needle is a marvel of engineering with some interesting features built in.

In this front view, you can see a long groove, running from the eye all the way to the thicker shank. This is designed to accommodate the thread as it pushes through the fabric. When the right combination of needle and thread is used, the fabric can't interfere with the thread in this groove.

Needle front view

In this side view, the indentation or *scarf* above the eye is visible. This is where the tip of the hook picks up the loop of top thread and pulls it around the bobbin case to form a stitch.

You can also see the flat part of the shank that allows the needle to sit properly in the needle clamp.

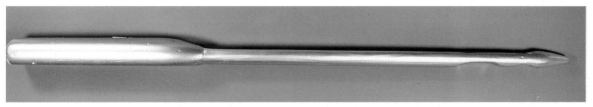

Needle side view

Important Relationships

A needle has two relationships. They are equally important, and understanding them will go a long way toward achieving great results.

RELATIONSHIP 1: NEEDLE SIZE AND THREAD

The size of the needle relates mostly to the weight of the thread being used. There is, of course, a correlation to fabric density, but the main relationship is between the diameter of the needle and the thickness of the thread. The thread must be able to hide in the long groove in the front of the needle as it goes down through the fabric. There should be no interference between the two in the front of the needle.

In the photo, you can see the thread as it is meant to fit into the needle. If the thread was thicker, then it would extend above the groove.

Front view of thread properly in groove

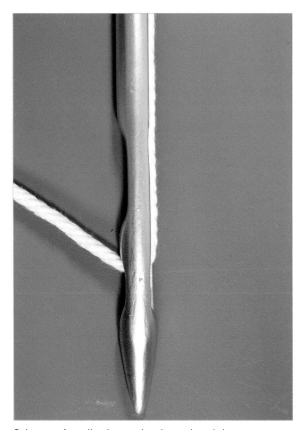

Side view of needle, showing barely any thread above groove

Thicker thread showing above groove

Now I'll explain why this is important.

FORMING STITCHES

When a needle pushes down through fabric, it takes with it a certain amount thread. This happens because the take-up lever on the front of the machine moves down at the same time, allowing slack in the upper thread. As the needle comes back up, the thread is pinched between the back of the needle and the fabric. This creates a loop above the eye at the scarf.

When the needle comes back up 2–2.5 mm, the tip of the hook grabs this loop, and as the top thread is pulled around the bobbin case, the take-up lever pulls the excess thread back up and snugly into the fabric. In the photo, my finger takes the place of the tip of the hook.

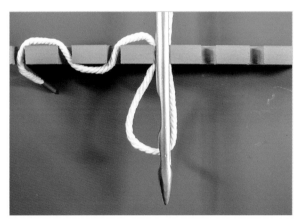

Loop formed

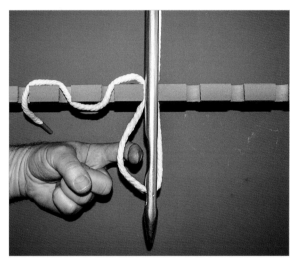

Hook grabbing top thread loop

If the thread is too thick for the needle, then the fabric interferes with the thread in the groove and creates a loop in front, above the fabric. This doesn't allow enough thread down through the eye to form the right size loop behind the needle.

The hook can miss the loop altogether and skip a stitch or hit the thread directly and break it. The stitches that are formed can give the impression that there is a tension issue.

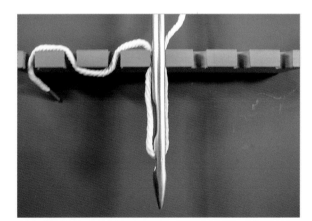

Loop in front, smaller loop in back

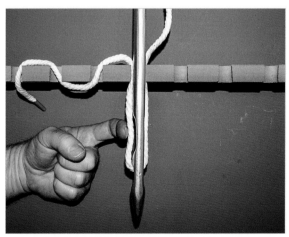

Hook missing loop

As you can see, this relationship between the weight of thread and size (diameter) of needle is very important.

NEEDLE SIZES

Needle packages are marked with the size on the outside. Typically, you will see 80/12, 90/14, and so on.

Needle sizes marked on packaging

The first number is a metric measurement of the needle diameter. A size 100 is 1 mm in diameter, size 80 is 0.8 mm, size 70 is 0.7 mm, and so on. This is a very easy to understand system. The second number is an American sizing number. In both numbering systems, as the number increases, the needle gets larger.

The larger the needle, the heavier a thread it can accommodate. The smaller the needle, the finer the thread.

SIZE OF THE NEEDLE HOLE

Another reason to use the correct size needle for the thread you are using is that the hole left by the needle can create what looks like a tension problem.

If you use a large needle with a fine thread, the thread will not fill the hole, and the loop of bobbin thread is easily seen, even though the tension is properly balanced. The stitches may appear slanted or staggered.

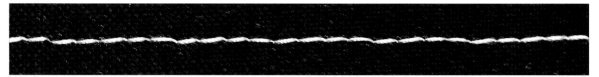

Fine thread with large needle

On the other hand, if you try to use a heavy thread with a fine needle, then not only are you risking skipped stitches and broken threads, but the top thread will not be able to pull the bottom one up into the hole created by the needle. This will look like the bobbin tension is too tight or the top tension is too loose.

Fine needle with heavy thread (top)

Fine needle with heavy thread (bottom)

Both samples above were sewn at the same tension setting.

As needles change in size, the length from the bottom of the eye to the tip may also change. This helps to keep an even taper as the needle diameter gets larger. The distance from the top of the eye to the top of the needle stays constant, so as not to affect where the hook grabs the loop.

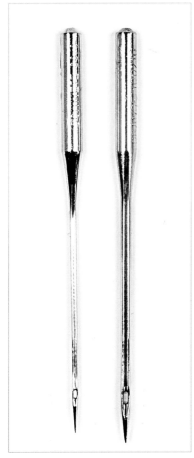

Needle length increasing with diameter

RELATIONSHIP 2: NEEDLE STYLE AND FABRIC

The point shape and style of needle relates directly to the type of fabric or, in some cases, the type of thread you are working with. Some needle manufacturers label the packages with names such as jeans, sharps, micro-tex, ballpoint, or leather, for example. These names usually refer to the type of point on the needle.

There are also specialty needles—such as quilting, topstitching, metafil, metallic, and stretch—in which a specific point is combined with other features to aid in sewing particular fabrics or specialty threads. These features may include a larger eye, special scarf (see Anatomy of a Needle, page 99), and special coatings.

TYPES OF NEEDLES

Ballpoint needles   True to their name, ballpoint needles have a rounded point. They are used to sew on knits, fleece, and other stretchy fabrics. The rounded point parts the fibers so they are not cut. This prevents runs in the fabric.

Jeans needles   Jeans needles used to be very sharp. In the last number of years, some manufacturers have changed this to what they call a *modified ballpoint*. This may be due to the fact that a lot of denim has become stretchy. It is important to note that if you are using finer jeans needles to do patchwork piecing on quilting cottons, which used to be recommended, you may now hear the needle popping as it pierces more densely wovens, such as batiks. This is because these needles are no longer sharp enough for this application.

Leather needles   A flat blade rather than a sharp point is the distinguishing feature of these needles. The sharp blade slices cleanly through leather rather than punching through. This makes it easier on the sewing machine, as there is less resistance.

Metafil or metallic needles   Metafil or metallic needles have a large eye and are recommended for metallic threads. They will also do a better job with monofilaments, including the flat, shiny decorative threads.

Microtex needles These needles have a very sharp tapered point and are used for tightly woven natural fabrics as well as microfibers. They are also the needles of choice for finer silks. The sharp point allows them to pierce cleanly with the least amount of resistance. The long fine taper makes it necessary to change them more often, as they are more easily damaged and worn.

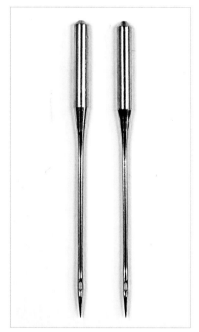

Universal needle (*left*) and microtex needle (*right*); notice long taper of microtex.

Stretch needles Stretch needles are a specialty version of a ballpoint. They have a modified scarf to allow for better pickup of the top thread by the hook. They are used on very stretchy fabrics, such as spandex or rib knits. They aid in preventing skipped stitches.

Topstitch needles These needles have a very large eye and are easier to thread. This large eye also reduces friction when using heavier and some metallic threads.

Quick or self-threading needles A small slot on one side allows the user to pull the thread easily into the eye of this needle. If you do not have a machine with a needle threader or your eyes are not what they used to be, these needles may be right for you. They are not to be used on dense fabrics, as they are structurally weaker. Also, the slot in the eye makes them unsuitable for batting and fabrics such as polar fleece, as fibers will get caught in the slot.

Quilting needles These needles feature a slightly rounded point and are recommended by their manufacturers for quilting with batting.

Universal needles Universal needles have a slightly rounded point and are the jack-of-all-trades but master of none.

LONGER-LASTING NEEDLES

Titanium-Coated Needles

These needles have a titanium coating that increases lifespan and are more glue resistant.

HLx5 Hard Chrome Needles

In my opinion, HLx5 needles (by Organ Needle Company) deserve some extra consideration. This is an industrial needle with a flat side in the shank so they will fit into your household machine. The hard chrome coating makes them last longer than regular needles. A specially designed shaft gives them less flexibility, which makes them less prone to deflection when doing free-motion work.

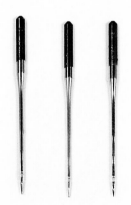

HLx5 color-coding

They are available in sharp and ballpoint, which covers a wide range of fabrics. The color-coding for size is helpful.

Choosing Needles by Quality or Price

If you are fussy about your stitching, buying quality needles from a manufacturer you trust is important. I often solve stitching problems just by changing needles. The needle is the least expensive thing you will buy for your project, and getting the right one of good quality makes a difference. I recently researched different brands for a distributor, and I took close-up photos of the groove in the front of the needle where the top thread lies. I was somewhat surprised to see how much smoother one needle was than another. The thread must slide in this groove, and I could see how much easier it was going to be in the smoother one.

It's easy to see which needle will give more consistent stitch quality.

To achieve good results, it is important that the eye of the needle be perfectly formed. This allows the thread to pass cleanly through without friction. I read somewhere once that the same piece of thread will go back and forth through the eye of the needle something like 93 times before becoming part of the seam. I have never counted, but it makes sense. Imagine the shredding and breaking (and frustration) if the eye is deformed or has a catch. The few pennies saved by buying a lesser-quality needle isn't worth the heartache.

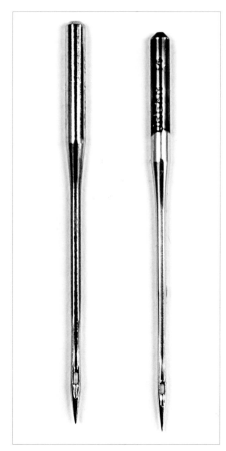

Comparison of groove

When to Change Needles

This is one of the most frequently asked questions. Often the needle will let you know by making a popping sound as it punctures the fabric. That sound can mean that the tip of the needle may be dull or damaged and the point is having a difficult time getting through the fabric. In this case, the fabric is probably being damaged. A damaged tip can occur when the needle hits the needle plate or the presser foot.

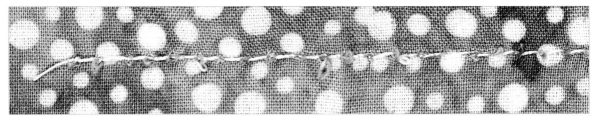

Damaged needle tip

Fabric damaged by blunt or deformed tip

It's also possible that you have switched fabrics and the needle is no longer the appropriate one for the new fabric. An example would be going from a knit to a woven cotton. If you were using a ballpoint needle and didn't change it, the needle will pop as it goes through the cotton.

If the machine is skipping stitches, it is a good sign that the needle may have to be changed. The skipping may be caused by a bent needle. The bend may be imperceptible, but enough to move the needle away from the tip of the hook as it comes by to pick up the top thread. The small gray bit represents the tip of the hook as it passes behind the scarf of the needle and picks up the loop of top thread.

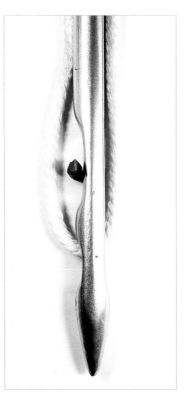

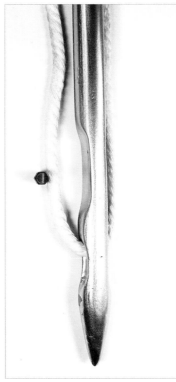

Normal position of tip of hook behind needle

Needle bent away from tip of hook

Having the wrong style of needle for the fabric you are sewing may also cause skipping.

As a guide, change needles ...

... if you hear a popping sound as the needle enters the fabric.

... if the machine is skipping stitches.

... if you change the weight of thread.

... if you change the type of fabric you are sewing (such as going from a woven to a knit).

... if the thread is breaking.

Important: When changing needles, it is important to have the flat part of the shank facing the correct direction. Almost all recent machines have the flat part facing the back. The exception would be the high-speed mid-arm machines that have the flat part to the right. Vintage sewing machines use a variety of positions. The rule of thumb is that the flat part is opposite to the needle bar thread guide.

The symptoms of having the needle in backward are broken thread and skipping stitches. Refer to your manual for the right position for your machine.

Make sure the needle is pushed up all the way to the stop in the needle clamp.

NEEDLE KNOW-HOW

I get many phone calls about problem stitching. Often before I explore any other options, I ask if the needle has been replaced with a new one. The answer is usually yes. When I get the sewing machine and see the problem is needle related, I find out the "new" needle was one sticking out of the pincushion. Now I specifically ask, "Is it a new needle out of the package?"

Something that I hear often is, "Use a real thick needle to sew thick fabric." Remember that a thick needle is for thick thread, and your sewing machine's motor may not have the power to drive a size 110/18 needle through denim. I have often hemmed jeans with a size 50 thread and a size 80 HLx5 needle. The sharp point, combined with a strong fine needle, went through the seams with no problem and did not strain the motor.

Summary

If you are noticing that there is some overlap in features of needles and feel that the differences are very subtle, you are not alone. It can be very confusing trying to figure out which needles you should buy. To simplify, if you have some sharps, some topstitch, and some ballpoint or stretch needles in various sizes, you will be well covered for different fabrics and threads.

Note: Remember the two relationships. The size or diameter of the needle with the thickness of thread and the type or style of the needle for the fabric!

Twin, Triple, and Hemstitch/Wing Needles

These needles allow you even more creativity! From hemming to decorative stitching to heirloom sewing, the right needle can be found in this group. Understanding their limitations and special needs will prevent and solve problems.

TWIN NEEDLES

Twin needles are two needles joined at one shank. They go into the machine just like a regular needle. Twin needles come with various points for different fabrics and various sizes for different threads. It is just as important to use the correct one as it is with regular needles (see Relationship 2: Needle Style and Fabric, page 103).

Earlier, left-needle-position machines had twin needles with a shank on the left side, but these are getting hard to find.

Twin needles come in widths from 1.6 to 8.0 mm. It is important to know your machine's limitations when it comes to these needles. If your needle plate has a 5 mm opening and you put in a 6 mm needle, you are going to hear a five-dollar "crunch" as one or both needles break on the foot or needle plate. Be sure to check the manual for your model to see the maximum width allowed.

Twin needles are used for hemming, pin tucking, decorative stitching, and even quilting. A 9 mm vertical hook sewing machine (see Sewing Systems and Hook Types, page 11) can take advantage of the widest twin needle. This can give you some of the nicest decorative stitching.

If you have a drop-in bobbin machine (see Sewing Systems and Hook Types, page 11), check your manual to see the widest needle allowed for your model. These machines use a horizontal hook, and the different needle positions are described in an arc, because the hook tip goes around in an arc. You can see this by the shape of the opening in the needle plate. It is possible that the very wide twin needles may hit both the plate and the hook.

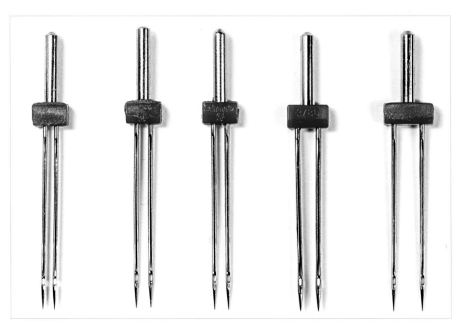

Various twin needles

TIP **Do the Math!**

When you are going to use a twin needle for any stitch that has zigzag in it, you must subtract the width of the twin needle from your maximum stitch width. Not doing this will result in a broken needle or even a broken presser foot.

For example:

9 mm max stitch width

– 3 mm wide twin needle

= 6 mm wide decorative stitch maximum

Twin needle about to hit foot

Some of you may have machines that let you tell them how wide the twin needle is and automatically override the width to its maximum allowable, whatever the stitch. This feature is well worth having and can save needles and damaged feet and plates.

Twin needle with proper width setting

For straight stitching, the twin needle width cannot exceed the width of the plate opening.

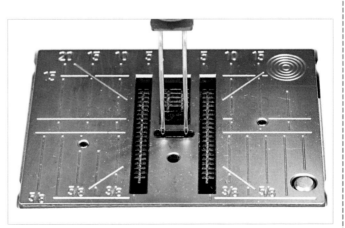

Maximum width twin needle for this machine

TRIPLE NEEDLES

A triple needle has a shank with three needles attached.

Triple needle

Triple needles can be used for topstitching, hemming, and some decorative stitching. As with twin needles, not all your machine's decorative stitches will look good when sewn with a triple needle. You will need to experiment to see what works.

Note: All the cautions that were listed for twin needles also apply to triple needles!

HEMSTITCH/WING NEEDLES

These needles are used for heirloom sewing and create holes in the fabric. They are sharp and can cut you, so be careful!

Hemstitch or wing needle

Because of the width of the blade, the stitch width will need to be adjusted to prevent needle breakage when doing any stitch with zigzag, just as you would with a twin or triple needle.

If you are straight stitching only, *do not* use a straight-stitch plate, as the needle may get stuck in the opening.

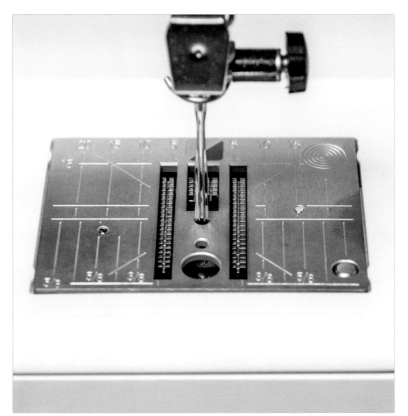

Wing needle stuck in straight-stitch plate

Machine Needle Threaders

Many sewists have a love/hate relationship with the needle threader. When they work, they are loved. When they don't, well ... you know. If it makes you feel any better, sewing machine technicians have the same feelings for them. If I had a dollar for every time I have fixed one of these devices, I would be retired and sailing to exotic ports to fix my boat.

The most frequently used phrase I hear is, "It's never worked!" This is probably because needle threaders are fragile, and it's easy to misuse them when a machine is new. The machines that thread completely automatically have a much lower frequency of threader breakdown because there is less human input.

How a Needle Threader Works

Whether the threader is activated by the sewist or automatically by the machine, they all end up doing exactly the same thing. A very fine wire hook is passed through eye of the needle from the back. This hook catches the thread, which has been put in its path in the front of the needle, and pulls this thread in a double strand, back through the eye.

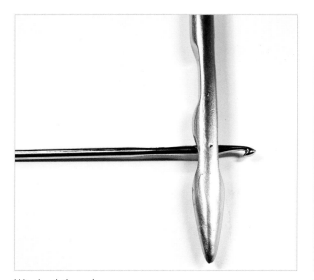

Wire hook through eye

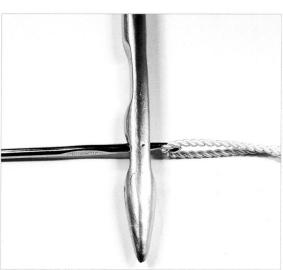

Wire hook with thread

What Could Go Wrong?

The threader mechanism is simple, but some things could go wrong. Let's look at those.

Needle in the wrong position   The fine wire must pass cleanly through the eye of the needle. If the eye is not positioned in exactly the right spot, the wire will come into contact with the shaft and bend. If you then reposition to the correct spot, the wire, being bent, will now pass to the left or right of the eye. This is when the name-calling starts and needle threaders are belittled!

Needle and eye in wrong position

Most machines that have needle threaders also have a needle-up-/-down button to choose where the needle stops. If you take a stitch before threading, then the machine has stopped in the right spot for the wire to go directly through the eye. Do not turn the handwheel by hand before using the threader. If you have set your machine to stop in the down position, then use the button or foot control to move the needle to the up position (see Turning the Handwheel, page 65).

Needle too fine   I recommend that you do not use the needle threader on a needle that is smaller than size 70/10. There is a good chance that the wire hook will get caught in the small eye on the finer needles. This will cause damage to the threader and may also scratch the inside of the eye of the needle, which will affect stitch quality.

Thread too thick for the needle   Relationship 1: Needle Size and Thread (page 100) discusses the relationship between thickness of thread and size of needle. This relationship also comes into play when it comes to the needle threader. The small wire hook must pull two strands of thread with it back through the eye of the needle. Considering the thickness of the wire itself plus the thread, the eye starts to fill up.

Two strands of thread in eye of needle

If the thread is too thick for the needle, the wire jams in the eye and can shred the thread or bend the wire hook.

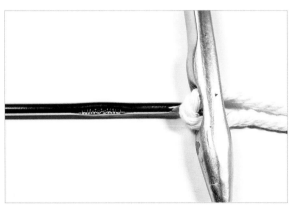

Thread too thick

This may also bend the needle back.

Lint in the threader head   Sometimes you've done everything right and the threader doesn't work as it should. Maybe it's intermittent or doesn't grab the thread at all. Lint buildup around the wire hook can prevent the threader from engaging all the way.

In this case, using a very fine pin and some tweezers, clean out the lint to make everything work again. *Caution: Do not dislodge any springs or wires.* Take a good look at how everything is put together first. If you are nervous about doing this yourself, your local sewing machine technician or shop would probably do this for you.

Inappropriate thread   Not all threads will work with your needle threader. Some plastic threads and some metallics are too stiff to pull gently through the eye of the needle. Also, some metallic threads have small extrusions that might interfere with the threader. These threads are best threaded manually.

Summary

A needle threader with a misaligned wire can cause damage inside the needle eye. This damage can cause shredded and broken threads. If you feel the wire catch in the eye, have your sewing machine technician do a proper alignment.

Always refer to the user manual for your model for correct use of your threader.

Automatic Thread Cutters

One of the great features on newer sewing machines is the automatic thread cutter. Now, at the touch of a button or a press on the foot control, your threads are cut. It can be a real time-saver. Some machines even raise the needle and the presser foot for you.

When you engage the cutter, a mechanism extends to grab the top and bottom threads and pull them into a blade with some pressure to cut them. This happens under the feed dogs. You will hear and see the machine move the needle to the appropriate positions. Let's look at what might cause problems.

Note: Oscillating-bobbin sewing machines (see Sewing Systems and Hook Types, page 11) do not have thread cutters.

Troubleshooting Thread Cutters

Lint and thread caught in the mechanism   The cutting blade has a pressure plate attached to ensure that as the thread is pulled into the mechanism, it is cleanly cut. If stray threads are caught, the pressure is reduced, resulting in erratic cutting. You might see a tattered thread end, or the thread might be cut only intermittently.

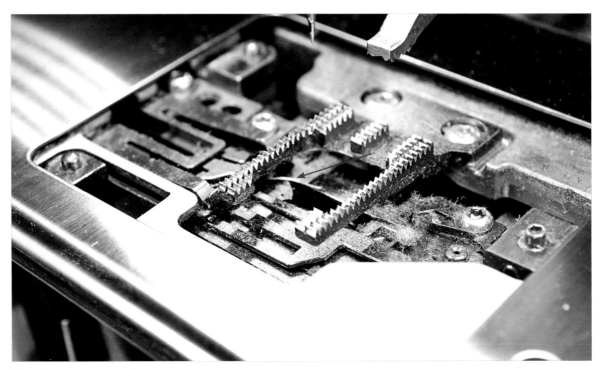

Thread caught in cutter mechanism

It is difficult to explain here how to clean all the variations in thread cutters offered by the manufacturers. If you feel that yours is not working well, start by taking off the needle plate (see Removing the Needle Plate, page 44) and looking for threads that are stuck. You can use tweezers to gently pry them loose. Some brands have a section in their settings area that will give you an icon to touch that will extend the cutter for easy cleaning. Refer to the manual for your machine to see specifically how to clean your cutter.

Inappropriate thread   Most cutters have no problem with the normal range of threads you might use. The exceptions that I have seen include thicker poly and Dacron threads, metallic, and some monofilaments. Thick cotton threads can also bog down a cutter. To extend the life of the blade and some of the rest of the mechanism, it is prudent to avoid using the thread cutter on these threads. You will probably know which ones overpower your cutter.

Dull blade   If you use the cutter a lot or use some of the threads mentioned earlier, eventually the blade will get dull and will need to be replaced. This is something your sewing machine technician should do, as there are alignments that need to be right.

Thread nest at beginning of seam after using cutter
There will always be a small nest under the fabric at the beginning of the next seam, after you have used the thread cutter. The top and bottom threads are cut at a precise length to leave enough thread to form a knot on your first stitch.

If you feel that the nest is too large, make sure that you are not pulling any extra top thread through the needle manually—this a habit that I see a lot. Just use the cutter and start sewing the next seam without touching the upper thread. This will give the smallest amount of thread behind the fabric.

TIP A Caution

↑ When cleaning the cutter area, clean gently. Do not poke a brush at it like it was a raccoon on your back porch. The reason I say this is that I have seen springs dislodged in the cleaning process. If you can't get the debris out with a gentle brushing and some tweezers, then I suggest you take the machine in to the shop and have it done there.

PRESSER-FOOT PRESSURE ADJUSTMENT

The presser-foot pressure adjustment is one of the most overlooked yet valuable features on a sewing machine. With it, you can adjust the downward pressure of the presser foot and ensure proper feeding on any fabric.

I have seen only a handful of sewing machines that have handled all fabrics without this feature.

Location of Adjustment

Most machines have a mechanical adjustment for pressure. It can be a dial on the side or top of the machine. It might have a number or graduating scale associated with it. The higher the number, the more pressure on the foot.

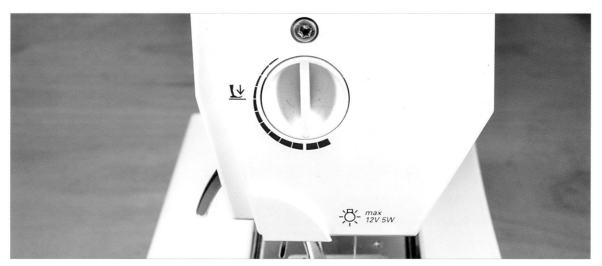

Dial on side of machine

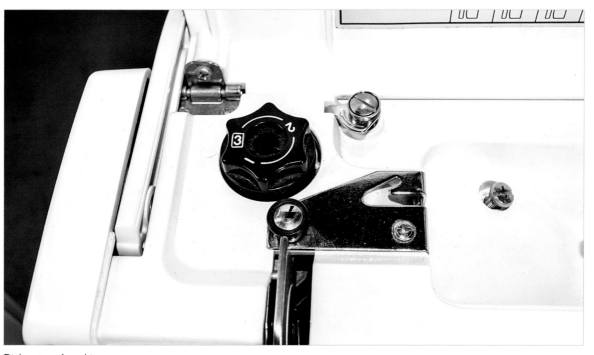

Dial on top of machine

Some vintage machines will have a button on the top left side of the machine. As the button is depressed, the pressure increases. Pushing down on the outer lower ring releases it. Some of the older machines may have an adjustment screw rather than the push-down button.

Button on left top of machine

Adjustment screw

Yet another style of adjustment is a lever inside the door that covers the take-up mechanism on the left side of the sewing machine. Move it down for more pressure and up for less.

Lever inside side door

Electronic Adjustment

Higher-end computerized sewing machines often have the pressure adjustment on a screen. For these machines refer to your instruction manual. These machines will often have different settings programmed in for different tasks.

Example of computerized adjustment

When to Adjust Pressure

Having a presser-foot pressure adjustment on your sewing machine gives you a much broader range of tasks you can handle without struggle.

Too Much Pressure

Something as simple as sewing two pieces of fabric together can be a problem if there is too much pressure. The top layer of fabric can end up longer than the bottom, and accuracy becomes more difficult. Imagine trying to piece a quilt under this circumstance. All the shifting and stretching of the top layer would make for a very wrinkly result.

Lowering the setting allows the top layer to be transported at the same rate as the bottom, and both layers end up the same length.

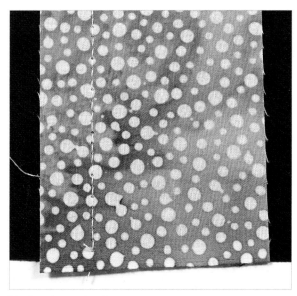

Top layer longer than bottom

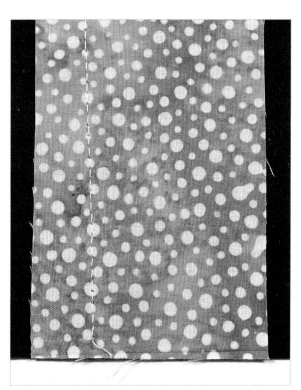

Both layers the same after adjustment

You can see the effect a simple adjustment can have. The samples were sewn on the same sewing machine at different pressure settings.

Another task for which too much pressure can cause a problem is sewing over thick seams, such as hemming a pair of jeans. When the foot gets to the thick seam, it starts to angle up in the front. If the pressure setting is too high, the foot might get stuck in this position and the fabric stops feeding.

Foot angled

In the best-case scenario, the stitches get much smaller; in the worst case, the feeding stops altogether, the needle breaks, or both happen.

Again, by lowering the setting, the foot is allowed to rise up easily at the seam and glide over. This takes away the struggle and minimizes changes to the stitch length.

Short stitch length at seam

After decreasing pressure

Not Enough Pressure

When there is not enough pressure on the foot and therefore on the fabric, you have another set of problems. The fabric floats, resulting in an uneven stitch length and wandering seams.

Seam with not enough pressure on foot; fabric floats.

The foot does not hold the fabric down as the needle is going up. This can allow the fabric to lift with the needle, resulting in skipped stitches and breaking threads. This can be a real problem when working with a free-motion or darning foot. The foot pushes down on the fabric when the needle goes in.

Foot down on fabric

As the needle lifts out, the foot stays on the fabric to prevent it from lifting until the needle is well clear.

Foot holding fabric down as needle lifts

Once the needle is high enough, the foot lifts, allowing easy movement of the fabric.

Foot lifts off the fabric

If you are experiencing skipping stitches or breaking threads when doing free-motion, increase the foot pressure so the foot can hold the fabric down properly as the needle is rising.

Summary

Presser-foot pressure adjustment is often overlooked as a cure for common problems. It is a most valuable tool and enhances your sewing machine's capabilities. A little study of your manual's chapter on this feature can give you new insight.

FORWARD/ REVERSE BALANCE ADJUSTMENT

Balance adjustment is a feature that is often ignored on sewing machines. It can play a significant role in how some of your stitches look.

Some stitches on your sewing machine move the fabric forward and backward. However, not all fabrics feed the same in reverse as they do in forward. The relationship between the length of the forward and reverse portions of these stitches is called *balance*.

The adjustment of balance changes the ratio of the length of the stitch between forward and reverse to allow the stitch to look as it was intended on a wide variety of fabrics.

Where Is the Adjustment?

The adjustment can be found in different places on different sewing machines. Some machines have dials located on the right side under the handwheel area. Your machine's manual will tell you where to find the adjustment.

On some computerized sewing machines, you will find a button on the front.

Push button adjustment on front

You may find the adjustment on your machine's touchscreen.

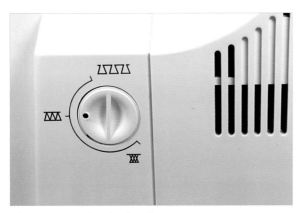

Adjustment on right side of machine

Others have a dial on the front.

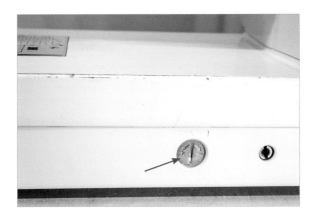

Adjustment on front of machine

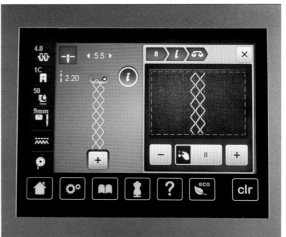

Touchscreen adjustment

When to Adjust

When you are working with a stitch that has a forward and reverse component and it does not look like the photo, it might be time for balance adjustment. The stitch may be piled up or stretched out.

Buttonholes

A very common example is with buttonholes, where the two beads are sewn in different directions. Often the forward and reverse beads are different stitch lengths. This results in an unattractive buttonhole.

By adjusting the balance, you change the relationship between these two beads to make them look alike.

Unbalanced buttonhole

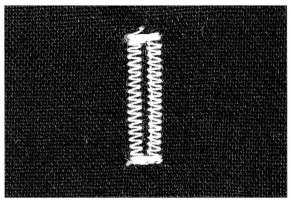

Balanced buttonhole—this buttonhole is much more pleasing to look at.

For more on making and troubleshooting buttonholes, see Buttonholes (page 128).

Stretch Stitches

These stitches are designed to stretch with knit fabrics. You will see that when using these stitches, the fabric moves forward and backward. This gives the seam elasticity.

Unbalanced straight stretch stitch

Stretch stitch after balance adjustment

Decorative Stitches

Many decorative stitches have a forward and reverse component. It may be necessary to adjust balance on some fabrics to give these stitches their intended look.

Unbalanced honeycomb stitch

After adjustment

Alphabets

If your machine has alphabets, you might find the need for balance adjustment. Letters come out nice and crisp when the setting is just right.

Unbalanced lettering

Perfectly balanced lettering

USING BALANCE TO CREATE A NEW STITCH

Your sewing machine may not have come with the perfect stitch for the job you are doing. Sometimes by adjusting the balance, it is possible to create that stitch. Here is a good example.

Recently my wife, Shelley, was teaching an appliqué class. She was after a stitch that would mimic hand appliqué, but the stitch designated for this on her machine had four stitches between the tiny zigzag that reached to the left to grab the appliqué fabric.

Mock hand-appliqué stitch with four stitches between

The gap was too big. What she wanted was a pattern that did one stitch between the tiny zigzags. The closest thing to this on her machine was the blanket stitch, but she wanted the zigzag portion to form a V.

Blanket stitch

By adjusting the balance, we were able to create exactly the stitch and effect she was after.

Blanket stitch after balance adjustment

The preceding photos show the stitching in contrasting colors to highlight the differences. In the next photo, you can see the stitch exactly as Shelley intended it to look on the project.

Newly created mock hand-appliqué stitch on project

Summary

I hope this chapter has helped you gain an appreciation for the value of the balance adjustment on your sewing machine. Not only can it help you solve feeding problems with certain stitches on some fabrics, but it can allow you to create new and different stitches. It is a very underrated feature!

BUTTONHOLES

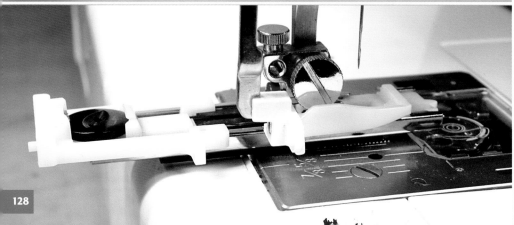

I have seen buttonholes cause stress in the relationship between the sewist and the sewing machine. A number of systems are offered by the different brands, and it's important to understand how yours works.

Buttonhole Systems

Dial with Buttonhole Stages

Early machines with built-in buttonholes had a completely manual system where the sewist turned a dial to engage the different stages of the buttonhole. Typically, these stages are ...

1. Bar tack (top of button hole)

2. Bead (line of stitching; down one side)

3. Bar tack (bottom of buttonhole)

4. Final bead (up the second side)

Most often, these types of buttonholes are sewn with the two long beads in different directions. It is not unusual that a balance adjustment is required to make these two beads look the same (see Forward/Reverse Balance Adjustment, page 122). Some sewing machines use a five-stage dial. This adds a tie-off at the end.

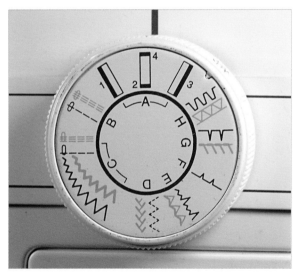

Typical four-stage buttonhole dial

Five-stage buttonhole dial

TIP Using the Correct Buttonhole Foot

On the completely manual system, to make a buttonhole where the two long beads are parallel, it is absolutely critical to use a proper buttonhole foot with the two grooves. The first bead rides in one of the grooves as the second bead is formed. This guides the fabric straight and keeps the two beads parallel.

Underside of manual buttonhole foot

Buttonhole made without proper foot

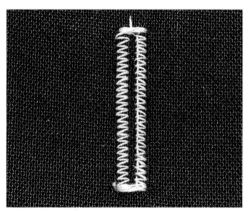

Buttonhole made with proper foot

Counting Stitches

Some sewing machines have programmable buttonholes that count the number of stitches in the first bead and then repeat that stitch count in the second bead. These machines can sew both long beads in different directions or in the same direction. If it is in different directions, one in forward and one in reverse, there is a possibility of over- or undershooting the bar tack.

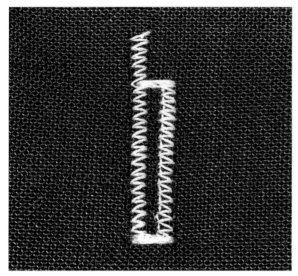
Overshooting bar tack

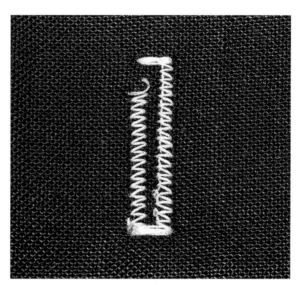
Undershooting bar tack

To help solve the problem, use a stabilizer under the fabric to help the fabric feed at the same stitch length in both directions. Ensure that the balance is correctly set (see Forward/Reverse Balance Adjustment, page 122).

Measured Length

Many sewing machines offer measured-length buttonholes. This is accomplished in different ways by the different brands.

TRIPPING A SWITCH BY LEVER

This is a very common system. The button sits in the foot and sets the distance to be measured. A lever is pulled down and rests between two tabs on the foot. As the foot is fed to the limits set by the button, the tabs engage the lever, which trips a switch that tells the machine when to bar tack and change directions.

Foot with button and lever pulled down

This style of buttonhole most often sews the beads in different directions. If the stitching does not look the same on both beads, a balance adjustment (see Forward/Reverse Balance Adjustment, page 122) may be required.

Sometimes with this type of system, the lever fails to trip the switch. This is a simple adjustment that can be performed by your sewing machine technician.

SENSOR FEET

Some brands offer feet that will measure the desired length of a buttonhole. These feet are used in different ways. Some sew the first bead, and then when the length is reached, the sewist touches a button to signal the machine to set the length. The buttonhole can then be repeated as often as needed without reprogramming each one.

Sensor type foot

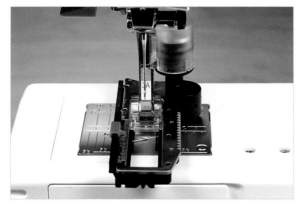

Sensor type foot

The foot recognizes when the desired length of any bead has been reached, and the machine takes necessary action.

INPUT BUTTONHOLE LENGTH DIRECTLY

Some machines allow you to enter the length of the buttonhole in millimeters directly. This, used in combination with a sensor foot, will give as many buttonholes of a given size as desired.

Enter buttonhole length.

Troubleshooting Buttonholes

Uneven Beads

For machines where the two long beads are sewn in forward and then in reverse, it is possible that the beads have different stitch lengths. To solve this issue, adjust the balance (see Forward/Reverse Balance Adjustment, page 122).

Sensor Foot Not Working Properly

If the foot is one that is plugged in, make sure the connection is positive.

If the sensor foot is the light beam type, make sure there is no lint or dust on top of the lens. Check also the lens in the machine, just above the one in the foot.

Sensor lens on foot

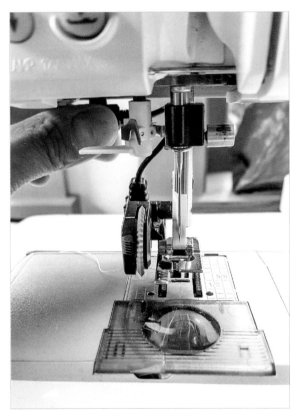

Sensor foot connection

Sensor lens on machine

This type of foot is also calibrated to its own machine. If you are the owner of two sewing machines that have this foot, it is easy to mix them up. If the buttonhole doesn't want to measure properly, try changing the feet.

Sometimes these feet can go out of calibration. On newer sewing machines from this brand, you can do this yourself. Just refer to the manual. On older versions, you will need to take the machine and foot in to the dealer for the calibration.

Fabric Not Feeding When Using Buttonhole Foot

There are situations in which the fabric may stop feeding when you are trying to make a buttonhole. When you are using one of the long buttonhole feet and it is resting on a ridge, such as at the edge of a jacket front, the feed dogs cannot reach the fabric properly to feed it.

There are two solutions to this problem. One is to turn the buttonhole and make it vertically. The other is called a *buttonhole compensation plate*. A number of brands have this kind of plate. It holds the fabric, and the machine actually feeds the plate.

Horizontal buttonhole across a ridge

Make buttonhole vertically.

Use compensation plate.

Fabric Puckering

A buttonhole is a satin stitch and as such, the fabric will tend to pucker. This is particularly true of the bar tack portions, as they are wider. To solve this, use an interfacing or stabilizer that is stiff enough to provide stability for the type of fabric you are using.

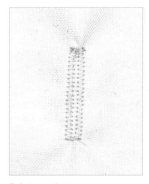

Fabric puckering

Fabric stabilized

MAKING GREAT-LOOKING BUTTONHOLES

Here are a few tricks to getting a nice looking buttonhole.

- Don't set the stitch length too short. The stitching can pile up and give a less-than-stellar result.

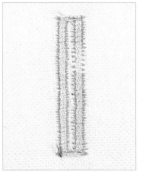
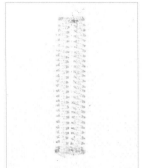

Stitch length short   Stitch length set a little longer

- Some sewing machines with oscillating hooks (see Sewing Systems and Hook Types, page 11) have a hole in the stitch finger of the bobbin case. Threading the thread through this hole will give a nicer-looking satin stitch and therefore a nicer-looking buttonhole.

Stitch finger threaded

Note: Do not leave the thread in this hole for normal stitching, as it increases the tension on the bottom thread and may not give the result you are looking for.

- Decrease the top tension. For those machines that don't have a way to thread the bobbin case, you can decrease the top tension to mock extra bobbin tension.

- Insert a cord into the satin-stitched beads of your buttonhole. Some feet are able to hold a cord as the needle stitches over it. This can make a very nice raised buttonhole. Just pull the loop in and snip the tails.

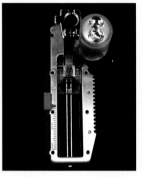

Cord held by foot   Corded buttonhole

- The type of thread you use and the amount of color contrast can make a big difference in how a buttonhole looks. A dark thread on a light-colored fabric can make a buttonhole look sloppy. A lumpy thread does the same. These were sewn at exactly the same settings and look quite different. Beauty, of course, is in the eye of the beholder and what works for you is right!

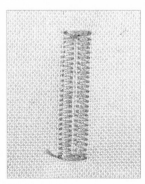

A lot of contrast   Closer match

TROUBLESHOOTING GUIDE

PROBLEM	POSSIBLE CAUSES	WHAT TO DO
	Bent needle	When to Change Needles (page 106)
	Needle in backward	When to Change Needles (page 106)
	Wrong needle for fabric	Relationship 2: Needle Style and Fabric (page 103)
	Damaged needle tip	When to Change Needles (page 106)
	Needle not pushed all the way up into needle clamp	*Push needle all the way to stop.*
	Needle too fine for thread thickness	Relationship 1: Needle Size and Thread (page 100)
	Too much basting spray	Using Spray Baste and Fusible Stabilizers (page 64)
Skipping stitches, shredding and breaking thread	Glue too sticky in fusible stabilizer	Using Spray Baste and Fusible Stabilizers (page 64)
	Not enough presser-foot pressure	Presser-Foot Pressure Adjustment (page 116)
	Thread getting caught somewhere in thread path	Wrong Size of Thread Stopper (page 87)
	Incorrect threading	Incorrect Threading (page 85)
	Old thread	*Change thread.*
	Damaged needle plate	Needle Plate Damage (page 88)
	Tarnished or damaged bobbin case	Damage to the Bobbin Case (page 82)
	Burr on hook	Smoothing Burrs on the Hook (page 80)
	Timing not set right	*Take your machine in for servicing.*
	Hook to needle distance off	*Take your machine in for servicing.*

PROBLEM	POSSIBLE CAUSES	WHAT TO DO
Loops on back of fabric	Machine threaded with presser foot in down position	How the Presser Foot Is Involved (page 69)
	Take-up lever not threaded	Missing the Take-Up Lever (page 85)
	Thread not in tension discs	Presser Foot Up (page 85)
	Thread or lint caught in tension discs	The Upper Part of the Machine (page 54)
	Burr on hook	Smoothing Burrs on the Hook (page 80)
	Damage on bobbin case	Damage to the Bobbin Case (page 82)
	Top tension set too low	Making Top Tension Adjustments (page 78)
	Thread too thick for needle	Relationship 1: Needle Size and Thread (page 100)
	Metallic thread too stiff	*Try a softer thread.*
	Tarnished metal bobbin case	Damage to the Bobbin Case (page 82)
	Thread is not supple enough.	*May be designed for hand stitching.*
	Thread too thick for sewing machine	Relationship 1: Needle Size and Thread (page 100)
	Knee resting on knee-lift lever when sewing	Knee Lifters (Free-Hand Systems) (page 19)
Inconsistent tension	Thread and needle mismatched	Relationship 1: Needle Size and Thread (page 100)
	Damaged bobbin case	Damage to the Bobbin Case (page 82)
	Burr on hook	Smoothing Burrs on the Hook (page 80)
	Tarnished bobbin case	Damage to the Bobbin Case (page 82)
	Wrong thread stopper	Wrong Size of Thread Stopper (page 87)
	Catch on outside edge of thread stopper	Wrong Size of Thread Stopper (page 87)
	Burr on hook	Smoothing Burrs on the Hook (page 80)
	Damaged needle plate	Needle Plate Damage (page 88)
	Damaged needle	When to Change Needles (page 106)
	Low-quality thread	*Use good quality thread.*
	Thread too stiff	*Try a softer thread.*
	High contrast in color between thread and fabric	What Could Go Wrong (page 76)

PROBLEM	POSSIBLE CAUSES	WHAT TO DO
Fabric won't feed	Not enough presser-foot pressure	Presser-Foot Pressure Adjustment (page 116)
	Lint buildup in feed dogs	Don't Forget the Feed Dogs (page 51)
	Damaged needle plate	Needle Plate Damage (page 88)
	Thread caught somewhere	*Remove thread.*
	Stitch length set too short	*Increase stitch length.*
	Walking foot lever not on needle clamp	Walking Foot (page 31)
	Presser foot damaged on underside	Chain Piecing with the Patchwork Foot (page 39)
	Knee resting against knee-lift lever	Knee Lifters (Free-Hand Systems) (page 19)
	Rubber feed dogs may be disintegrating	Types of Feed Dogs (page 23)
	Feed dogs down	Dropping the Feed Dogs (page 24)
Uneven stitch length	Incorrect pressure on presser foot	Presser-Foot Pressure Adjustment (page 116)
	Presser foot worn underneath	Chain Piecing with the Patchwork Foot (page 39)
	Wrong foot for job	*Change presser foot.*
	Lint buildup between feed dogs	Don't Forget the Feed Dogs (page 51)
	Heavy fabric needs more support	*Help fabric to feed.*
	Pulling fabric	*Guide fabric without pulling.*
	Pushing fabric	*Guide fabric without pushing.*
	Rubber feed dogs may be disintegrating	Types of Feed Dogs (page 23)
	Walking foot lever not correctly mounted on needle clamp	Walking Foot (page 31)
Won't climb seams	Too much presser-foot pressure	Presser-Foot Pressure Adjustment (page 116)
	Wrong foot	Using the Right Foot (page 29)
	Seam needs to be flattened	Going Over Heavy Seams (page 64)
	Feed dogs not all the way up (some older machines)	Dropping the Feed Dogs (page 24)
	Lint buildup in feed dogs	Don't Forget the Feed Dogs (page 51)
	Stitch length set too short	*Adjust stitch length.*

PROBLEM	POSSIBLE CAUSES	WHAT TO DO
Fabric puckering	Tension too tight	Tension in the Relationship (page 67)
	Stabilizer required	Fabric Puckering (page 135)
	Wrong needle plate	Needle Plates (page 17); Needle Plate Damage (page 88)
	Needle point damaged	When to Change Needles (page 106)
	Wrong needle for fabric	Relationship 2: Needle Style and Fabric (page 103)
	Top thread hung up somewhere in thread path	*Rethread machine.*
	Not enough presser-foot pressure	Presser-Foot Pressure Adjustment (page 116)
	Thread too heavy for fabric	*Change thread.*
Needle hitting	Bent needle	*Change needle.*
	Pulling fabric	*Guide fabric without pulling.*
	Pushing fabric	*Guide fabric without pushing.*
	Wrong presser foot	Using the Right Foot (page 29)
	Wrong needle plate	Needle Plates (page 17)
	Top thread caught	Wrong Size of Thread Stopper (page 87)
	Drop-in bobbin case has spun around	Missing the Take-Up Lever (page 85)
	Timing out	*Take your machine in for servicing.*
Noise in bobbin area	Hook needs lubrication	Lubrication (page 57)
	Damaged plastic drop-in bobbin case	Drop-in Bobbin Case (page 83)
	Bent needle hitting hook	*Change needle.*
	Tarnished metal bobbin case	Damage to the Bobbin Case (page 82)
Machine jammed	Thread caught in hook	Thread Lock (page 97)
	Lack of lubrication	Lubrication (page 57)
	Use of inappropriate lubricant	Using the Right Oil (page 57)
	Thread cutter jammed	Automatic Thread Cutters (page 114)
	Thread caught and wrapped around handwheel	*Unravel thread.*
	Thread caught in take-up mechanism	The Upper Part of the Machine (page 54)

PROBLEM	POSSIBLE CAUSES	WHAT TO DO
Machine won't turn on	Cord not properly plugged in	*Check cord placement.*
	Fuse blown after needle hitting	Safety (page 16)
	Fuse blown after thread jam	Safety (page 16)
	Damaged power cord	*Replace cord.*
	Surge protector turned off	*Turn on surge protector.*
	Problem with power print	*Take your machine in for servicing.*
Erratic on high speed only	Burned contacts in rheostat	Rheostat (page 20)
	Grease or debris on resistor of electronic foot control	Foot Controls (page 20); Electronic (page 21)
	Blown capacitor in foot control	Erratic Speed (page 21)
Low-bobbin sensor not working	Lint in sensor area	Bobbin Sensors (page 52)
	Damaged bobbin	Damaged Bobbins (page 96)
	Wrong type of bobbin	Using the Right Bobbin (page 72)
	Using prewound bobbins	Prewound Bobbins (page 72)
	Bobbin door open while sewing	*Close bobbin door.*
	Malfunctioning sensor	Bobbin Sensors (page 52)
Upper thread warning comes on	Lint or thread in sensor	*Clean thread path.*
	Incorrect threading	*Rethread machine.*
	Sensor activator has jumped out of check spring	*Take your machine in for servicing.*
	Sensor malfunctioning	*Take your machine in for servicing.*
Machine is on and makes buzzing noise but won't sew	Bobbin-winder activating lever may be engaged	*Disengage bobbin winder mechanism.*
Thread nest after using cutter	Pulling extra top thread after using cutter	Thread Cutter (page 114)
Buttonholes won't feed properly	May need compensation plate	Troubleshooting Buttonholes (page 134)
	Stitch length may be set too short	Making Great-Looking Buttonholes (page 136)

INDEX

ABOUT THE AUTHOR

Bernie Tobisch was born in Germany and moved to Canada as a young boy. He grew up in Saskatchewan and moved to Alberta in his early twenties, where he began his career as a sewing machine technician with Singer. He became a dealer after a few years and continued to service machines. In the late 1980s, he moved to the Vancouver region, opened up shop, and has been there since. He has a daughter, Bonnie, and son, Gord. He also has one grandson, Dylan, whom he thinks would make a great technician!

Bernie is happily married to his wife, Shelley. They met in the sewing machine business and have worked together for the past 20 years teaching classes on precision piecing, machine quilting, and getting to know your sewing machine. He also still services sewing machines.

Bernie enjoys sailing and fishing, and if he ever retires, he would love to sail off into the sunset to repair his boat in exotic locations!

AUG -- 2018

Want even more creative content?

Go to ctpub.com/offer

& sign up to receive our gift to you!

Make it, snap it, share it
using
#ctpublishing

For a list of other fine books from C&T Publishing, visit our website
to view our catalog online.

C&T PUBLISHING, INC.

P.O. Box 1456
Lafayette, CA 94549
800-284-1114

Email: ctinfo@ctpub.com
Website: ctpub.com

Tips and Techniques can be found at ctpub.com/quilting-sewing-tips.

For quilting supplies:

COTTON PATCH

1025 Brown Ave.
Lafayette, CA 94549
Store: 925-284-1177
Mail order: 925-283-7883

Email: CottonPa@aol.com
Website: quiltusa.com

Note: Fabrics shown may not be currently available, as fabric
manufacturers keep most fabrics in print for only a short time.

**/THING**

*you need to know to keep
your sewing machine happy*

For any brand of sewing machine

Written by an expert sewing machine technician with over forty-two years of experience

Learn how your sewing machine works, how to keep it happy, and how to troubleshoot common problems

C&T PUBLISHING

11272   **US $24.95**
ISBN-13: 978-1-61745-581-0
52495

9 781617 455810

Also available as an eBook